EXTENDING THE BOUNDARIES

For our own team:
Melanie, Jack, Nathan, Carly, Tamsyn and Caja

EXTENDING THE BOUNDARIES

Theoretical Frameworks
for Research in
Sport Management

Allan Edwards

Keith Gilbert

James Skinner

COMMON
GROUND

This book is published at theLearner.com
a series imprint of the UniversityPress.com
First published in Australia in 2002
by Common Ground Publishing Pty Ltd
PO Box 463
Altona, 3018
ABN 66 074 822 629
www.theLearner.com

National Library of Australia Cataloguing-in-Publication data:
Edwards, Allan, 1953– .
   Extending the boundaries : theoretical frameworks for
   research in sport management.

   Includes index.
   ISBN 1 86335 107 8 (pbk.).

   ISBN 1 86335 446 8 (PDF).

   1. Sports administration. 2. Sports – Research. I.
   Skinner, James, 1964– . II. Gilbert, Keith, 1950– . III.
   Title.

   796.069

Cover designed by Diana Kalantzis.
Typeset in Australia by Common Ground Publishing.
Printed in Australia by Mercury Printeam on 80gsm White Bond.

Contents

Acknowledgments

Many different individuals have contributed to the writing of this book. Indeed, when we first began to read so that we would better understand the conceptual basis and theoretical frameworks for the individual book chapters several important people came together to discuss the work and comment on its use in the higher education context. Thanks therefore go to, Professor Nicola Yelland, and Professor Karin Volkwein-Caplan who provided us with valuable feedback so that we could cut through the theoretical haze and get to the relevant material in order to simplify the nature of the task.

We would like to thank our postgraduate students who critiqued chapters and added to the debate in classes and seminar series, which were organised over the two-year period of writing. In particular we would like to thank Melinda Richards, Hafidz bin Haji Omar, Louise Schuller, and Andrea Davidson whose comments were insightful and poignant. Dr. Jarrod Meerkin of the Australian Paralympic Committee Sports Science Research Coordinating Centre was especially helpful as the main reader and we found his comments encouraging and perspicacious. In particular, we would like to thank Professor Otto Schantz from the University of Strasbourg who provided invaluable support when commenting on and pointing out the shortcomings of our arguments. He was able to advise us from a background where the European traditions and constructs have been deeply ingrained in cultural discourse and already characterised by the volatile relationship between theoreticians. This provided us with a stronger comprehension of the problems, which we would encounter later when attempting to place the theoretical concepts in the sport management domain.

Almost all of our research was carried out in our respective Australian university libraries and we received great support from the staff that continually sent papers and books through the inter-library loan service. Most of our research was tested and discussed with undergraduate students from Griffith University, Gold Coast Campus, Southern Cross University, Lismore, Queensland University of Technology and Monash University and much of our thinking and reflection took place in these classes. To all of our students at the universities over the years we appreciate your willingness to engage in constructive debate and to argue through the issues and assist in the development of our own thinking regarding the theoretical areas.

Thanks also go to all those people who spent countless hours placing the contents of our book into manageable print ready format. More especially we would like to thank Janet Huntley for her editing support in the early writing phase and Linda Singh for the final draft editing and text development. On a personal front we would like to mention the support, which we received from our families and thank them, as we believe that they have over the years supported our professional development, and in doing so, aided our personal ambitions. As authors we have become closer as our friendship has developed and through our continual debate we have hopefully been able to place the theoretical constructs in this book into some form of manageable framework. In doing this it is hoped that all might understand the basic premises of the difficult concepts, which we struggled with in the initial phases of the development of the text. All three of us are aware however, that this book represents the beginning of a journey into the unknown, which will not be completed until we have further enriched the sport management profession, and perhaps more importantly cultivated and stimulated debate and controversy.

About the Authors

Dr. Allan Edwards is a lecturer at Griffith University, Gold Coast campus. His research interest focuses on postmodern methodology and reflective practice. He is researching in the area of culture and surfing with Surfing Australia and the International Surfing Association. Dr. Edwards has strong links with the Australian sports industry in particular the Australian Rugby league, Queensland Rugby Union, Professional Golfers Association (PGA) and the Australian Paralympic Committee.

Dr. Keith Gilbert is an Executive Board Member of the International Council of Sport Science and Physical Education and was the Assistant Chef de Mission (Administration) for the year 2000 Australian Paralympic Team. Dr. Gilbert is an academic at Monash University where his research interests include the Sociology of Sport and in particular the use of qualitative research methodologies.

Dr James Skinner is a lecturer in sport management at Southern Cross University. His doctorate utilised postmodern theory in examining the influence of global commercial forces on the strategic direction and culture of Queensland Rugby Union, the governing body of rugby in Queensland. He has an extensive publication record in sport management. His primary research interest is in culture as it relates to change and sporting studies. James has delivered numerous seminars and workshops nationally and internationally on a variety of sport management issues.

Foreword

Sport is not what it used to be. For many sport followers this is cause for lament. For example, Alan McGilvray, Australia's leading cricket commentator during the 1970s and 1980s, concluded that the 'game was not only 'not the same'; it had also lost much of its intrinsic value. According to Alan, this sorry 'problem' was directly related to its growing commercialisation.

There is no doubt that sport has been transformed over the last 30 years. At the elite end of the sport continuum it has become a complex commercial enterprise, while at the 'participation' end, it has become quite sophisticated in marketing its activities to local communities. As a result, a variety of professional skills are required to manage sport in all its forms. This, in turn, has produced a plethora of higher education programs in sport management.

Sport management is now a respectable academic discipline. It has its own peer-reviewed journals, higher degree programs, international conferences, and research agendas. More higher degree students than ever before are undertaking research programs, and an increasing number of government grants are being allocated to sport management issues.

However, the one area where sport management studies are underdeveloped is research design. Researchers, for the most part, have been forced to access the generic management literature for their theories and conceptual frameworks. In many respects this has not been a bad thing, but it often means that some of the 'nuances' and special features of sport are not given sufficient focus. The book 'Extending the Boundaries: Theoretical Frameworks for Research in Sports Management' fills a significant research gap by customising the discussion to the sport management researcher. This is a particularly exciting development.

Allan Edwards, Keith Gilbert, and James Skinner have produced a very impressive guide for researchers who wish to study sport in an organisational setting. Not only have they taken a number of esoteric postmodern theories and 'unpackaged' them for us, but they have also directly linked them to the study of sport organisation and management. This difficult task has been performed admirably by the writers.

Postmodernism has become a fashionable academic paradigm, but is rarely discussed in a clear and concise manner. Its inaccessibility to many is compounded by its proponents using the works of writers like Michel Foucault and Jacques Derrida to mask their own partial understandings of postmodern thought. Allan, Keith and James have all used postmodern theory to frame their own research projects, and they are consequently able to both demystify the theory and use it to inform their discussion of research into sport management. This is one of the book's major strengths.

Allan, Keith and James have produced a unique and ground-breaking work. The have brought together a number of valuable research designs, ranging from critical ethnography and action research to deconstruction and discourse analysis. In each case they provide a concise guide to how each model can first, be applied to sport management issues and problems, second, strengthen the research design, and finally, enhance the research process.

I recommend this book to experienced and novice researchers alike. I have no doubt it will open up rich and rewarding fields of sport management research.

Dr. Bob Stewart
Associate Professor of Sport Management
Victoria University
Melbourne, Australia

Introduction

The discipline of sport management has probably been the area least affected in recent times with the postmodern condition and as such there are few books or journal articles written in the discipline of sport management, which highlight the meaning of the term and all things associated with it. However, whether we like it or not we are stuck with the term postmodernism for as Shapiro (1990) remarks 'for better or worse the term 'postmodernism' has entered the general language of our culture'. Indeed, even though it has become a household word, most academics in the sport management field have, as yet, not established an understanding of the nature of the 'postmodern condition' or its meaning.

We are arguing, consequently, that social scientists and other academics in the profession of sport management who rarely use the term or infrequently write the term into their journal articles or book chapters require a text, which highlights the major nuances of the difficult, and demanding theoretical constructs associated with the postmodern condition. Our belief is that this difficulty occurs principally because many academics are unenthusiastic about learning and understanding the postmodern condition due in part to their difficulty in interpreting its theoretical and practical use in the research arena. In discussion with many of our peers we were surprised to hear that they were concerned about the long-term effects of the introduction of postmodern ideas into their research methodology. Thus, we discovered that these foreshadowed theories have been left out of mainstream research in our field and have therefore not been subject to abject criticism and lively debate. One of the main premises for the writing of this text was to encourage and develop debate and in doing so this book will hopefully then create change, provide further critical analysis and open our field to new, interesting and fresh research developments.

In order to contemplate writing in the area and becoming involved in confusing and often seemingly needless controversy the academic in the area of sport management could do worse than at least have a limited understanding of the issues which have plagued the academic world over the past two decades. After all, the genre of writing and theoretical considerations have the ability to take academics in the field 'out of their comfort zone' and force them 'kicking and screaming' into the new millennium. However, when we asked other academics about the problem we found them to be mostly disinterested. We then asked ourselves the question; how can this book provide a better understanding if certain individuals in higher education are not interested in the theories and epistemological nature of contemporary research into the 'postmodern condition'? Other questions arose; was it just a matter of the academics being accustomed to their own well-researched methodologies and theoretical structures, which elucidate their research? For instance, when writing this book we came to understand that as researchers we need to continually enhance our appreciation of the literature and how text works in providing an instrument to enable us to offer differing perspectives on the research process. This we realised could only be achieved by assisting the researcher to become a critic and be more objective in their development of theory.

We also realised that time is an important factor in the development of research projects in today's world of higher education and that the best way in which we could collectively develop other academics understanding of the 'postmodern condition' was by writing and attempting to simplify the process of understanding. We do not mean to denigrate or in anyway attempt to cause others to think that we are elitist in our thinking but just to simplify the process of understanding. In doing this we have aimed to develop a text as a reader for undergraduate and postgraduate students, as well as interested staff in the higher education sector.

This book therefore places the theories and structures into context within the nature of sport management so that others can utilise the theory and mingle and mix the emerging genre. Along with these thoughts we believe that the new genre will be heterogeneous as its individual and contemporary usage can be developed across a level and range of research activities which have their own distinctive discourses and epistemology's. In short, we believe that although we have developed this text in the context of sport management research the theories herein can be applied to all forms of social science research.

In many ways then, we are offering solutions to emerging problems in the world of sport management research, which are highlighted in the context of culture. This is manifest in our understanding of culture which we discovered can be developed by the use of a particular theory or mix of theories which in turn can be utilised to view the problems thrown up by the research project in a different light. Thereby developing the field and the understanding of the researcher as to the role which theory plays in the context of research. Postmodernism can thus be the cornerstone of new and exciting ways of developing our postgraduate students thinking and analytical skills because an analysis of postmodern texts always leads to research questions which lead to further conceptualisation and understanding of the problems which lead to further research projects. In many ways we discovered that the development of new and exciting theoretical concepts were really grounded in the historiographical basis of our previous work and that utilising cross cultural theory enabled us to better understand the nature of our work and future research directions. For us the discovery of this New World has brought about a major paradigm shift and a major developmental stream to follow. In particular the development of 'postmodern research fashion' has effortlessly crept into our lives at a time when others have discarded the process or arguments have been briefly discussed as to the importance of the area to sport management. Indeed, it is fair to state that although all three of us have experimented by utilising separate theories we are by no means expert in all. However, we would hope that this text would encourage others to develop and follow a particular strand or theory so that we might develop our field in the future in new and exciting directions. What follows is an attempt to set the record straight, to place the postmodern condition on the research agenda and to determine new directions for sport management research.

Chapter one discusses the nature of ethnographic research and highlights the benefits of post-modern ethnography as an appropriate and emerging methodology for sport management research. It reviews the positivist tradition and argues for the interpretive alternative. It elucidates the differences between anthropological ethnography and functionalism and the theoretical constructs of symbolic interactionism, ethnomethodology and grounded theory. In particular it argues that the centrality of power is important in the context of sport management research. We were concerned by the notion of the researcher as a subject and attempt to position the researcher as a neutral gatherer of data while developing the notion of voice and the development of the text in ethnographic research. In doing this the chapter develops and argument for the use of emerging ethnographies such as critical ethnography, but in particular postmodern ethnographic research.

Chapter two offers an acute analysis of the nature of postmodernism and sport management research. The examination of post structuralism and postmodernism and its implications for the future of research in the area achieve a theory practice mix, which strengthens our thoughts and ideas regarding the development of the area. If anything, we provide a framework for the remainder of the chapters and add new strength and vitality to the sport management area. This chapter suggests a number of historical and theoretical reasons for the longevity of the postmodern paradigm and the need for academics to be cognisant of the immersion of power into the vernacular of popular sport management research. In supporting these ideas we highlight the characteristics, problems and meanings of postmodernism by placing the theory into the context of sport management and contemporary sport management.

Chapter three argues that critical theory has emerged as an important issue in the development of sport management research. Throughout this chapter we have attempted to explain the meaning of critical theory and the origins, which encompass the realms of social theory, and the differing schools of thought. In particular the Frankfurt School of critical theory and how its theoretical constructs can be developed into strong support for sport management research. It observes the thoughts of Habermas and how he reflected the characteristic distrust for positivism or scientism. The chapter also views the end of critical theory as a paradox which enables organisational and sport management research to exist amidst the technologies of the New World. In particular, the chapter supports the notion and use of critical theory in future sport management research.

The notion of deconstruction is dealt with in chapter four which deals principally with the ideas espoused by Derrida and the extrapolation of signs and significations from texts. It questions and raises important principles in relation to the truth and understanding of textual content and the significance of deconstruction in sport management research.

Chapter five is an attempt to focus on the socio-cultural and political context in which discourse analysis can be utilised in sport management research. When arguing for a Foucauldian perspective we note that the approach is useful for the examination of differing discourses. In this chapter we discuss the term discourse and argue that it has a particular meaning for sport management research. Again we take a Foucauldian perspective which is developed into a 'new order' of thinking about language and support the notion of 'the division between true and false'. We then follow the Foucauldian perspective of discourse analysis, which is again reflected in the notion of power/knowledge transition. The last section of the chapter reviews discourse and the importance of sport management research by arguing against the 'taken for grantedness' of specific sport management practices. The chapter is arguably one of the most important in the book as it supports the role of sport management theory as a form of discourse. This in turn is supported by the notion of sport policy as discourse so that the reading of texts that represent certain viewpoints can actually be analysed and developed as viable research projects.

Chapter six reviews the notion of 'action research' as an interesting variation for research projects in the area of sport management research. We note that 'action research' is already a part of management research but that it is not readily understood in the context of sport management theory. We define the term and identify the five features of action research and then develop the origins and the notion of emancipatory, practical, and technical 'action research'. An examination of the generations of action research and the characteristics and limitations is achieved by developing differing interpretations that contain their own set of assumptions. Throughout the chapter we describe the different epistemological assumptions that underpin the generations of action research and discuss the implications for sport management research. It finishes with the support of the principles of action research in new research traditions and directly relates the issues involved to sport management research.

Chapter seven argues through the constructs of reflective practice by critically examining the debate into the potential contribution to sport management research. We develop the definitions and origins of reflection by supporting the view of Schon (1983) who argues that reflective research should be in terms of 'knowledge in action'. Furthermore, we examine the 'Dimensions of Reflection' and the challenges to reflection while arguing through the notions of critical theory and reflective practices. The theory practice divide and the use of reflective practices in sport management research provides basis for a rationale for further research. It finally links the concepts of action research and reflective practices by providing an empowering and emancipatory role for the research in the context of professional practice and expertise. We argue that forms of reflection provide a unique opportunity to understand the practitioner's world and provide further opportunities for emancipatory practice.

Chapter eight argues that there is need to distinguish between narrative and story telling, however, they we suggest that they both have an important role to play in sport management research. The authors put forward the case that narrative is a useful a way of approaching the world of sport management research. They go on to add that it is a useful a tool, and in many ways as useful to date as more scientific approaches. However, they caution that these claims will carry little weight if these crucial terms are employed so loosely within the field. 'Story' is informal, provisional and exploratory. 'Voice' however, means the distinct epistemology of a social, professional and political group and 'Narrative' should mean the consciously formulated, premeditated and coherent account of an experience. When defined in this way the authors suggest that 'narrative' involves the recognition of its author as capable, self-defining and intellectually able individual.

To summarise, this book examines the usefulness and discusses the 'postmodern condition' and the areas of theoretical interest, which spin off the condition. Principally, the volume is attempting to achieve something innovative while also opening up a new area of research for the sport management profession. In this manner we have included chapters, which challenge the very core of sport management research and articulate the meaning of the theories in a sensitive veneer of postmodern prose. Finally, we would like to note that as reflective authors we are open to new and innovative suggestions, which we feel could benefit research in the field of sport management. Let's challenge convention not just live it.

Chapter 1
Research Traditions

Theory must always be the central and irreducible goal if sociology is to take a significant place within the development of human self knowledge.

M. Waters (1994: 1)

The Positivist Tradition

The positivist research tradition in sport management grew out of the view that social scientists should use research methods that were similar to those which had seemed to lead to the discovery of objective laws and regularities in the natural sciences. There is in this tradition therefore a concern with measurement, reliability, prediction and replicability. The appropriate way of going about knowledge production is thought to be by means of the hypthetico-deductive method in which the researcher begins with a clearly articulated theory, deduces hypotheses which are logically consistent with the theory, and then tests the hypotheses under experimental conditions. But since social science hypotheses do not often lend themselves to laboratory experimentation, statistical analysis of large samples usually counts as objective testing. Such methodology assumes that through observation and precise measurement, social reality, which is external to and independent of the mind of the observer, may be rendered comprehensible to the social scientist.

It is in approaches to theorisation, as much as in the methodology itself, according to Sharp and Green (1975), that the 'inherent weakness' of such deductive research is revealed. Critical social theorists have attacked the positivist, logical empiricist tradition. They argue that while 'fact finding' and 'head counting' produces voluminous statistical data, it does not address the social circumstances out of which such data arise. Quantitative, positivist sport management studies assume the existence of a natural social order with an underlying value consensus. According to Sharp and Green, this limits both the formulation of problems to be studied and the conceptualisation of possible solutions:

Methodologically, this tradition tends to engage in positivistic 'fact finding' procedures with arbitrarily imposed categories for differentiating the data. It fails to do justice to the complexity of social reality, which cannot be 'grasped' by merely reducing sociologically significant characteristics of men to their external and objective indicators. (pp. 2–3)

In the positivist tradition, or paradigm of social science research (Kuhn, 1962), emphasis is placed upon the search for generalisations or laws, which will enable not only explanation but also the prediction of social behaviour, and therefore social intervention and control (Berstein, 1978; Fay, 1975). Fay further indicates that by treating conventional activities and social circumstances as if they are naturally occurring entities, the positivist approach reifies the social institutions and customs of the society it is studying. By reification, Lukacs (1971) explains that social arrangements are treated as if they were immutable things that must necessarily be the way they are. Social structures and the structural relationships are regarded as inevitably functioning the way they currently do regardless of the wishes of the social actors. Research, which reifies social arrangements in this way by treating them as neutral, cannot be ideologically neutral itself; as such research must necessarily implicitly endorse such arrangements and lend support to the status quo. Positivism, therefore, can be viewed as excessively narrow and inflexible.

The Interpretive Alternative

Criticism of the separation of the individual from social structures, which is a characteristic of the positivist tradition, coupled with a philosophical attack upon the tenets of positivism, and the realisation that social advances do not necessarily follow any correct scientific manner (Kuhn, 1962), led to the emergence of more interpretive research (Woods and Hammersley, 1977). This approach shares a common concern with the investigation of ways in which human actors themselves construct the social world through the interpretation of the interaction with other human actors. This approach is especially apparent in the development of other versions of ethnography.

Anthropological Ethnography and Functionalism

Although, as Smith (1987) reports, the evolving field of ethnography is in a state of 'zesty disarray', the essential feature of most ethnographic research is that it attempts above all to describe 'the nature of social discourse amongst a group of people' (Wilcox, 1980, p.2).

This viewpoint is most apparent in the American tradition of ethnography with its particularly strong roots in anthropology (Delamont and Atkinson, 1980; Spindler and Spindler, 1971). Ethnography is regarded by such researchers as the 'science of cultural description' (Wolcott, 1975, p.112), a means by which to understand what it is like to 'walk in someone else's shoes' (p. 113).

Geertz (1973) whose influence upon such cultural ethnography has been important, regards ethnography as 'thick description' which locates the multi-layered significance of events within their social contexts. Since the most significant data amount to 'our own constructions of other people's constructions of what they and their compatriots are up to', analysis involves 'sorting out the structures of signification' (p. 9). The researcher must therefore be in a position to observe behaviour within the context of its setting, and to elicit from those observed the 'structures of meaning which inform and texture behaviour' (Wilcox, 1980, p.2).

The latter point raises the important question of the extent to which conventional ethnography has actually allowed a shift from the view of human nature, which is an integral part of the positivist, structural-functionalist paradigm (Burrell and Morgan, 1979). Indeed, especially in the American tradition of largely anthropological ethnography, an essentially limited, structural-functionalist approach to human nature and society is still apparent despite the use of methodologies that are thought to afford understanding through description and interpretation.

Although offering some insight into the day-to-day reality of human life, such ethnography only provides the perspective of an interested observer.

Sociological Ethnography, Symbolic Interactionism, Ethnomethodology, and Grounded Theory

While the American tradition of ethnography derives largely from anthropology with emphasis upon the understanding of events, the use of ethnography in Britain has been associated more with sociology. In this tradition this emphasis has been more upon an understanding of relationships rather than activities, and research has been based more explicitly upon sociological theory.

Sociological ethnography derives particularly from symbolic interactionism, which attempts to explain how the definition of the situation is negotiated amongst a group, and from ethnomethodology, which seeks to understand the social construction of reality. In both cases, concern is with social interaction as a means of negotiating meanings in context.

In contrast to positivism, the emphasis in the interpretivist tradition, with its roots in symbolic interactionism and ethnomethodology, is upon the elucidation of 'the way in which the social world is constituted by the actors' meanings' (Freeman and Jones, 1981, p.1). Both symbolic interactionism and ethnomethodology place human actors and their interpretive and negotiating capacities at the centre of analysis. Their common phenomenological perspective reflects an attempt to understand the world through the subjective perceptions and meaning of its human actors. Researchers working within a symbolic interactionist framework actively enter the world of the research subjects. They continually move between social theory and the world of people who are the subjects of the research, between their conceptual framework and the immediate social experience being studied (Denzin, 1988).

Grounded theory method, with its aim to develop explanatory theory concerning common life patterns, has emerged from the symbolic interaction tradition. The specific techniques within grounded theory method were originally developed and refined by Glaser and Strauss. Their book, *'The Discovery of Grounded Theory'* (Glaser and Strauss, 1967), presents these strategies for qualitative research to the work of human science research. In doing so, Glaser and Strauss shared their notion that this was a 'beginning venture in the development of improved methods for discovering grounded theory' (p. 1). Also, their basic position, in contrast to logical deduction theory building from a priori assumptions, was 'that generating grounded theory is a way of arriving at theory suited to its supposed uses' (p. 3). Thus, theory building is based on the accumulation of data that reflect the experiences of the researcher.

In ethnomethodology, attention is also upon human actors and the way in which members of various social groups make sense of the social situations in which they find themselves. The influence of ethnomethodology in the sixties and seventies emphasised the rule-governed negotiation of intersubjectivity, the mutually defining emergence of structure in process and process in structure. Ethnomethodology facilitates a process in which its primary focus is 'the meaning and understandings that people use to make sense of their everyday lives' (McNeil 1990, p. 94). This methodology is substantively continuous with the phenomenology of ethnography.

What has defined the character and trajectory of ethnography in the past quarter century has been its theoretical eclecticism. In other words, ethnographic practice has been driven by a diverse and competing range of methodologies borrowed from phenomenology, symbolic interactionism, ethnomethodology, Marxism and feminism. Most recently, critical theory and postmodernism have attracted the attention of researchers. They have been particularly useful in providing greater theoretical weight to ethnographic research.

Emerging Ethnographic Research

In this section, it will be argued that critical ethnography and postmodern ethnography can address the weaknesses that exist within the positivist and traditional approaches to ethnography. These forms of ethnography, while taking advantage of the advances of traditional ethnography over positivism, depart from the traditional approach to ethnography in a number of significant ways.

Power and the Researcher as Subject

Critics of traditional ethnography are concerned about the exclusion of power from the field of study. Recent interpretive analyses has drawn attention to the role individuals play in the construction and maintenance of meaning systems, and hence constitute 'a vast improvement' upon work by positivists and structural functionalists, however, it fails to address the power relations between these individuals.

Habermas (1978) suggests that traditional ethnography lacks a theoretical relationship to the political practices that might bring about emancipation of the people being investigated. Conventional or traditional ethnographic description uncritically represents versions of perceived realities without locating its stories within a framework of political and social explanation. Far from intentionally enlightening the subjects of an ethnography or giving them the means to understand and alter their circumstances, traditional ethnographic practice has historically involved subjective, anthropological description in which the subject of ethnography is observed by an authoritative, yet sympathetic, observer (Hammersley, 1992; Weedon, 1987).

Fay (1975) argues the traditional approach of ethnography is inherently conservative because, in assuming that actual social practice is inherently rational and that conflict is due to irrational understandings, it endorses change that leaves the system in tact. Hence, traditional approaches that seek to be interpretative by nature, would only 'lead people to seek to change the way they think about what they or others are doing, rather than provide them with a theory by means of which they could change what they or others are doing' (p. 91). Such a theory would draw attention to the interrelationship between knowledge as beliefs and attitudes, actions and power relations, and by doing so offer a social, rather than individualistic, approach to the question of change.

Another area of concern is the apparent negation in traditional ethnography of the role of the researcher in the construction of the data they present. Gitlin, Siegal, and Boru (1989) and Tyler (1983) draw attention to the textual practices of interpretive ethnographers that, they argued, deny the voice of the researcher-as-author. While the researcher may describe their initiation into the field, the subsequent identified social or cultural patterns are present as objective descriptions, untainted by either the ethnographers' presence or the rhetorical decisions made. Tyler maintains that such:

> ... ethnography is a textual practice intended to obscure its textual practices in order to present a factual description of the way things are, as if they had not been written and as if an ethnography really were a picture of another way of life. (p. 84)

As Marshall (1989) notes in his critique of objectivism in educational research, 'such a presentation of the world as an external reality implies that it can be observed objectively and impartially by any person' (p. 104). The ethnographic picture and the researcher are positioned as independent entities. This style of narrative realism presents fieldwork as an essentially rational activity rather than a social and political undertaking.

In positioning the researcher as a neutral gatherer and hence the presenter of truth, traditional ethnographies are seen to deny the notion that knowledge is constituted within social relations. The researcher is not understood to be implicated in the production of the knowledge that purportedly belongs to the informants. Indeed, while the context of the research may be understood as socially constituted, the researcher is not, they are presented as a neutral tool.

Critical Ethnography

Critical ethnography constitutes an alternative to traditional ethnographic research. As well as emphasising the inherently ideological nature of the social sciences and their part in governing contemporary capitalism, critical ethnography attempts to reconstruct the conceptual practices that comprise ethnography. Consequently, accepted canons of ethnographic practice, such as grounded theory, the use of (borrowed) analytical concepts such as validity, generalisability and so on, have either been rejected or reformulated. Although this approach is still in its nascent stages, the implied critique of grounded theory within the approach of 'extended case method' (Burawoy, Burton, Ferguson, Fox, Gamson, Gartell, Hurst, Kurzman, Salzenger, and Schiffman, 1991), Anderson's (1989) concept of a 'critical reflexivity', or Smith's (1987) notion of 'entry points' within the everyday, have suggested the emergence of a coherent, viable, alternative research programme(s) to that of traditional ethnography.

In contrast to traditional ethnography critical ethnography acknowledges the existence of power relations in the construction of meaning systems. By acknowledging this existence it seeks to emancipate its subjects through enlightening them to the political and social circumstances of their existence. As critical ethnography seeks to be emancipatory, its subjects by definition are constrained by oppressive social or political relations of some kind. Critical ethnography becomes the public voice for groups within society who might otherwise remain voiceless.

Although exponents of critical ethnography agree that research conducted the traditional ethnographic mode is concerned with social change, and recognises the political nature of knowledge production and its process of legitimation, differences exist in their understanding of the actual research agenda as well as their theoretical orientation. For some, the research process itself constitutes, in part, the intent of the study. Such work is concerned to directly empower research participants, including the researcher, through joint critical reflection on the constitution of their interpretive frameworks. This process involves exploration of the discursive positions from which participants are speaking and the creation of spaces from which the marginalized are heard. Therefore, empowerment of the marginalized is not a product of the work of the researcher who, as the 'transformative intellectual', assists participants to realise the falsity of their views and to adopt the use of the researcher's critical discourse or that of a new-shared reality. Rather, empowerment involves the research participants in an exploration of the politics of production of their knowledge.

However, although critical ethnography talks about the empowerment of individuals involved in the research process and alerts to us to particular types of issues of injustice, it does not actively involve the researcher in empowering the research participants' understanding of the research issue under investigation.

Postmodern Ethnography

The contribution of postmodern ethnography to empirical work on organizational behaviour to date has been minimal. According to Kilduff and Mehra (1997), this is because organizational researchers tend to neglect or reject the critiques of academic enquiry offered by those who write from a postmodern perspective. They suggest that this might be because the import of postmodernist approaches for organizational studies is unclear. Indeed the term postmodern is itself vaguely understood: it is often equated with deconstruction (Linstead, 1993), and is generally viewed as a nihilistic enterprise that offers nothing beyond a cynical scepticism (Codrescu, 1986). Nor are the works of such authors as Derrida, Foucault, and Baudrillard, who are often associated with the postmodern turn, accessible to the majority of those practising organizational research. Postmodern writings are therefore derided for their unintelligibility (Thompson, 1993), and dismissed for reducing research to textual analysis (Giddens, 1987).

Within social sciences in general the spectre of postmodernism has aroused widespread anxiety. Kilduff and Mehra (1997) suggest that:

Postmodernism has been viewed as an enterprise that calls for the death of all scientific enquiry; the end of all new knowledge; the dissolution of any standards that may be used to judge one theory against another; a banishment into utter relativism wherein a clamour of fragmented and contentious voices reign. (p. 454)

In practice however, postmodern ethnography as in critical ethnography challenges the content and form of dominant models of knowledge, and also produces forms of knowledge through breaking down disciplinary boundaries and giving voice to those not represented in dominant discourses (Giroux, 1992). However, postmodern Ethnography moves beyond critical ethnography in that the presence of the researcher is encapsulated in the research. The researcher is actively involved not only in the research process, but also in the empowerment of the research participants' understanding of the research issue under investigation.

To achieve this, Kilduff and Mehra (1997) argue that postmodern researchers, in pursuit of conventional wisdom, can mix and match various perspectives of research styles for aesthetic effect in order to contrast with tradition (p. 458). This freedom to combine styles of discourse follows from the belief that no method grants privileged access to truth and that all research approaches are embodied in the cultural practice that postmodernists seek to make explicit (Smircich and Calas, 1987).

Paramount in the postmodern shift is a re-examination of the values, beliefs, and practices perpetuated by elites that serve to suppress the expression of minority viewpoints. The importance of finding a single totalitarian truth or commonality is replaced by the realisation that multiple truths exist simultaneously and that the real issue is not what the truth is but which one is being allowed to be heard. By focusing attention on social processes like power and conflict, which operate below the surface of an individual's awareness, postmodernism challenges the monopoly of currently dominant orthodoxies.

Hargreaves (1994) in his conclusions drawn about postmodernism suggests that 'adapting a postmodern theoretical position involves denying the existence of foundational knowledge on the grounds that no knowable social reality exists beyond the signs of language, image and discourse' (p. 39). The implication of this, according to Hargraves, is that 'all that is available to the postmodern theorist is the practice of deconstructing existing versions of social reality, and giving voice to other versions which are normally neglected or suppressed' (p. 39). Thus, deconstruction constitutes a postmodern method of analysis that examines the basis of how an author comes to privilege a theory or version of reality that is considered superior to others.

As a result the context, content and methods of entire research disciplines have become more open than ever before to continuous rethinking, reanalysis and reinterpretation. The works of 'experts' who were heretofore considered major contributors are being examined for biases attributable to their membership in dominant groups. The views of critics deconstructing the grand narrative (which attempts to account for a range of phenomena in terms of a single determining factor) and providing a voice to the marginalized are being given increasing hearing and weight. In short, research is witnessing an explosion of reflexivity, wherein 'accepted' interpretations of the past are being increasingly challenged for their relevance.

Hargreaves (1994), however, implies that deconstructing grand narratives and giving voice to the marginalized, in themselves are not sufficient for the research process. According to Packwood and Sikes (1996), there is a danger that research methods and approaches that solely reflect personal experiences and emotions of the researcher can lead to self-indulgence and narcissism rather than to enhanced understanding and useful ways of viewing the world. They suggest that in order to eliminate this trap, it is essential to situate deconstructions within their social, political, economic and moral contexts. In these instances it is possible to apply postmodern approaches when they are appropriate and when they offer the opportunity to take a more critical stance towards aspects of the research process and the area being studied.

According to Packwood and Sikes (1996), what postmodernism has to offer is a focus on the narrative of the individual and the acknowledgment of the situated, partial nature of knowledge claims within the context of the shifting and often contradictory nature of reality. In other words, the meta-narratives that comprise single explanations for the occurrence of a phenomenon are to be deconstructed into micro-narratives of the individuals. This approach serves a dual purpose. First, it allows the voices of those dispossessed by meta-narratives to be heard. Second, it allows the taken-for-granted truths and realities of those meta-narratives to be made problematic and therefore verified. Consequently, the researcher needs to be cautious of broad universal claims and remain open to diverse interpretations through the inclusion of alternative representations.

Such an approach however, may be construed as moving towards an abstract representation of reality. Tyler (1987) refuted this and suggests postmodern ethnography does not move toward abstraction away from life, but back to experience. It aims to restructure individual experiences and restructure the conduct of everyday life. Postmodernists therefore, prefer the interesting to the obvious and place a high value on paradox, contrast, counter intuition, and humour (Fine and Martin, 1995). From a postmodernist research perspective there is no point establishing the obvious through laborious research. Such research not only brings social science into disrepute with its publics (thus violating the postmodernist emphasis on relevance), but also wastes resources on research questions that simply confirm what everyone knows (Kilduff and Mehra, 1997). Postmodernism, then, involves a search for the non-obvious, the counterintuitive, the surprising, the ambiguous, the contradictory, and the chaotic.

In scientific research there is a search for wholeness and interconnectedness rather than the fragmentation of phenomena. In sport management research modern methods of scientific examination and expert-driven discourse could be supplanted by postmodern methods of conversation that allow the emergence of multiple realities and the realisation of the limitations of currently dominant paradigms. The postmodern approach therefore views the narrative as a dialogical production of a cooperatively evolved polyphonic text. In other words, it can be representative of the differing views that exist in any sporting organization. Utilising this approach allows the researcher to capture the fractured and chaotic reality of organizational life, and its varying impact throughout the sport organization.

In conclusion, as the swell of critical/postmodern thinking disrupts cherished practices of research, the foundations of ethnographics tradition have come under critical scrutiny. Traditional ethnography's imperative of revealing the insider's reality has been plagued with problems. Discourses of the natural, of science, of objectives and subjectivity that variously intersect to produce ethnographic method are being contested in the light of more recent discourses such as postmodernism. Postmodernism broadens the field of ethnography by accentuating awareness of research practices, drawing attention to the role of power relations in the construction of reality, problematising the role of the researcher as subject, and empowering the research participants understanding of the research issue under investigation.

Concluding Comments

The story of ethnography is currently being rewritten. As the swell of postmodern/critical thinking disrupts cherished practices of research, the foundations of ethnographics tradition have come under critical scrutiny. Positivistic and quantitative approaches to sport management research (Auld, 1997; Cuskelly, 1995; Shilbury, 1994) have historically dominated the discipline in Australia. Qualitative methods, and more recently the support for emergent ethnographic approaches to management research (i.e. Hardy and Clegg, 1997) provide an alternative to the positivistic testing of formal theories developed by empirical researchers. While qualitative research has not been universally embraced in the general discipline of management, it is gradually evolving into a more accepted practice in the specific discipline of sport management. The recent works of Edwards (1999), Kellett, (1999), Skinner, Stewart & Edwards (1999) and commentary by Chalip (1997) provide a clear indication of this.

This chapter has discussed the strengths of emergent ethnographic research and its applicability to a sport setting. It proposes that a postmodern ethnographic case study can provide a voice for those organizational members whose opinions can be suppressed by powerful individuals. This approach allows the researcher to capture the full impact of organizational life and is therefore an applicable research design. In doing so, this chapter has aimed to break new ground by encouraging a move away from the historical domination of the positivist tradition in sport management research in which data comes mainly out of surveys and questionnaires.

As sport management academics grapple with questions regarding the nature of the knowledge that informs their discipline, it is important that they assess particular research practices before they adopt them. Failure to do so may lead them to unwittingly generate knowledge that is inimical to their particular quest. The emergent ethnography discussed in this chapter offers academics and others interested in the generation of knowledge, not only a methodology that invites the possibility of opening up previously hidden areas of sport management practices, but one that actively involves the researcher in challenging their taken-for-granted assumptions.

Chapter 2

Postmodernism and Sport Management Research

...postmodernism is a state of things which challenges and transforms existing hierarchies in all spheres of contemporary life.

Smith & Wexler (1995: 2)

The Origins of Postmodernism

In order to have a grasp of postmodernism we felt that we needed an understanding of the concept of modernism and we gained this from the work of Harvey (1989) who in his wide ranging book, '*The Conditions of Postmodernity*', reminds readers that while pre-modernity reaches back into antiquity, the Renaissance may be considered the passage way to modernity.

In this manner we realized that 'Modernity' was therefore directly associated with the 'age of enlightenment', that began in the eighteenth century in Western society. Harvey (1989 pp 12–13) also noted that 'the age of enlightenment' developed 'human creativity, scientific discovery and the pursuit of individual excellence in the name of progress', and furthermore supported, 'doctrines of equality, liberty, faith in human intelligence and universal reason'.

He does however, go on to describe the numerous 'anti-modernist' movements as having sprung to life by the 1960s, and their anti modernist perspectives spilling over into the streets 'to accumulate in a vast wave of rebelliousness' on a global scale, later in 1968.

One of the products of this disenchantment was the birth of more localised political action groups, like the environmental and feminist movements, with single-issue objectives, which were not tied to any particular political ideology. This growth in 'micro-political formations' was also accompanied by styles of theorising, which in an analogous way were antagonistic towards totalising tendencies. Forms of grand theorising that focused on abstractions like class and ideology, and which critical theory is prone to perpetrate, were frowned upon. This new social theory, most of which has emanated from France rather than Germany, has been given a variety of names—the most common being postmodernist or poststructuralist theory.

Consequently, the initial critique of modernity came from a poststructuralist perspective. Poststructuralists rejected the assumptions and 'scientific pretensions' of structuralism and positivism which according to Best and Kellner (1991) sought the standard modern goals of 'foundation, truth, objectivity, certainty and system'.

Poststructuralism had its beginnings in European, particularly French, philosophy. Until the late 1960s French philosophy was divided between the individualistic theories of phenomenology and existentialism on one end of a continuum and collectivism theories dominated by Marxism on the other. In opposition to both of these, cultural structuralism, inspired by the linguistics of Levi-Strauss and Barthes, and Freudian psychoanalysis arose in the mid 1960s. Structuralism challenged both phenomenology and orthodox Marxism by dethroning the sign from the centre of meaning and displacing consciousness from the centre of subjectivity (Smart 1993). Structuralists advocated a formal system of analysis with rules and conventions that provide a way of examining interactions between the system and its individual elements, in the case of sociology, the social practices by which society and culture relate to and govern the individual. Poststructuralism goes even further by putting language at the centre of social reality. Indeed, rather than reflecting reality poststructuralists argue language creates it. Poststructuralism then links language, subjectivity, social organization and power in the context of modern thought. Poststructuralists, including Foucault, Lyotard, Baudrillard, Deleuze, Guattari and Derrida undermine all previous assumptions and make all knowledge's, including structuralism, problematic. According to Smart (1993) poststructuralists:

> ...call attention and contribute to the crisis of representation. They reveal the fragile and problematic representational character of language, the disarticulation of words and things and the ways in which meaning is increasingly sustained through mechanisms of self-referentiality and thereby deny us access to an independent reality. (pp. 20–21)

One of the aims of poststructuralism, therefore was to challenge the authority of established discourse by 'deconstructing' (Derrida,

1976) the linguistic organisation of the subjective self and social institutions, identifying how signifying and discursive practices empower and privilege certain individuals, groups, and forms of social life.

Poststructuralist theorists have criticized the theoretical and ontological adequacy of the 'meta-narratives' of philosophy—the metaphysical conception of subjectivity, truth and reality'. What separates poststructuralist theories from critical social theory is the opposition to the notion that the subject is a free and creative source of meaning and asserts, instead, that language constructs the individual's subjectivity in ways that are socially specific.

However, power in critical social theory is understood in terms of forces that subordinate and dominate. Poststructuralists regard the construction of the 'self' as an effect of power, a view of power that is central to the work of Foucault. He proposed a link between knowledge and power relations, referred to as 'knowledge/power', that govern understandings of knowledge and truth. Power is conceived as a motivational force, not driven by the law or the state. It is not centralized, but operates at the 'material, physical and corporeal' level of everyday existence. It is understood as something exercised to sustain rights and impose duties. It is productive as it gives rise to practices and techniques. This productive action of power relates to the ways in which the subject is integrated into a particular body of ideas or ways of knowing (White, 1988, p. 190).

The terms poststructuralism and postmodernism are often used interchangeably but they are not identical concepts. Poststructuralism has been interpreted as a subset, of postmodernism, which is viewed as a broader range of, theoretical, cultural and social tendencies (Best and Kellner, 1991). Postmodernism offers a sociohistorical perspective whose discourse entails a more detailed analysis of postmodern society. As with poststructuralists, postmodernists turned to discourse theory to explain how meaning is socially constructed semiotically using codes and rules in signifying practices.

The postmodernists claim that fundamental sociohistorical changes cannot be adequately explained by modern theories, therefore new conceptual schemes are required. Postmodernists favour social analysis that incorporates local, conceptualized and restricted conceptual strategies that have an explicitly practical or moral interest. Local natives are preferred to ground narratives, telling local stories rather than articulating general theories.

Although postmodernism is a broader, more inclusive concept than poststructuralism it is now more readily accepted as 'a fait accompli' that the words can legitimately be used synonymously (Smart, 1993).

Defining The 'Postmodern'

The term 'postmodern' has a variety of (contested) usages. Firstly, in philosophy it refers to critiques and theories typified by Foucault (1970), Derrida (1976) and Deleuze and Guattari (1994). They stress the plural, fragmentary and subjective nature of reality and of the self. Secondly, in the arts it refers to a negation of the 'modern' movements in painting, architecture and literature, and a focus on the power and nature of representational systems within culture. Thirdly, in social studies it refers to social and political transformations in the western world brought about by 'post-industrialization', information technology and the breakdown of consensus politics (Callinicos, 1989; Harvey, 1989; Layder, 1994). It is the first usage that this chapter is mostly concerned about.

Postmodernism is currently characterized in the international literature in inconsistent and even contradictory ways. According to Hudson, (1989, p.140) it is characterized (inter alia) specifically as:

- a myth
- periodization
- a condition or situation
- an experience
- an historical consciousness
- a sensibility
- a climate
- a crisis
- an episteme
- a discourse
- a poetics
- a retreat
- a topos
- a task or project

However, for cynics, the only discernible point of consensus amongst postmodernists is their lack of consensus on postmodernism. Some regard it as a continuation of modernism (Sherry, 1991), others consider it to be a complete break with the past (Venkatesh, 1989). Some draw distinctions between postmodernism, postmodernity and postmodernization (Featherstone, 1991), others treat the terms synonymously (Jencks, 1987). Featherstone (1988) for example, expands upon a family of terms derived from these two generic concepts. Specifically, he contrasts 'modernity and postmodernity', 'modernization and postmodernization' and 'modernism and postmodernism'. On deploying these terms Featherstone notes how the prefix 'post' seems that which comes after.'

Thus as a critique of modernism, postmodernism represents a realisation that there is not single truth but multiple realities, all are legitimate and all equally valid; that individuals, societies and economies are not governed solely by instrumental reason but are subject to historical and cultural processes that cannot be explained by reason alone; and that the human being is not necessarily the center of the universe; that modernism is itself a egregious male oriented conceptualisation of the world and has consistently retarded female participation in human affairs (hence the emergence postmodern feminism). It states that capitalism is not the only desirable form of economic order; that progress does not mean marching linearly toward a predetermined goal; that the quality of life need not be measured in economic and material terms only; and that in human affairs aesthetic judgment is just as important as economic judgment. (Venkatesh, 1992, p. 19)

In his discussion of the theoretical and critical position of postmodernism, Eagleton (quoted in Harvey, 1989, p. 9) proposes that it:

> ...signals the death of such 'metanarratives' whose secretly terroristic function was to ground and legitimate the illusion of a 'universal' human history. We are now in the process of wakening from the nightmare of modernity, with its manipulative reason and fetish of the totality.

The postmodern condition can therefore be seen as 'incredulity towards metanarratives'; in other words a refusal to accept that there is one particular way of doing things and that one way only will achieve the desired results.

Knowledge is thus seen as being always provisional, and relative to the context of its generation. It is therefore also essentially incoherent and contradictory, and self-reflexive within and through its generative cultural context. Postmodernity thus rejects all claims to certainty, and all transcendental timeless truths and meanings. Knowledge is also viewed as being legitimated consensually and autonomously within its particular cultural context. There is a rejection of heteronomous or foundational legitimation theories, wherein recourse is made to a universal foundation of truth, such as reason, nature, or the will of God. Rejected then are the traditional grand narratives, theories or philosophies of legitimation, whether they be of an empiricist, rationalist, Marxist or other viewpoint. By extension, postmodernity involves a rejection of grand universalizing social or development theories or schemata. It is anti-canon, in the sense of rejecting the idea that any intellectual tradition has epistemologically privileged authority.

The postmodernist skepticism towards all claims to the privileging of knowledge is perhaps important in conditioning the postmodern mood. Its point is that any claim for a superior path to what is true, good, or beautiful—whether it be rationally, spiritually, empirically, or otherwise based—is to be regarded with the utmost suspicion; with a profound skepticism even a cynicism. Indeed, any claim to the privileging of knowledge is seen as being open to use or abuse by its protagonists as grounds for intolerance towards that which is privileged. Abuses of the system are seen as underpinning the cultural genocide, which from a postmodernist perspective characterizes the history of modernity. It denies a priori superiority not only to any path to knowledge, but also to knowledge claims themselves. It thereby also denies that there are any a priori substantive grounds for privileging one set of beliefs over others.

Problems with Postmodernism

What then are we (especially as sport managers) to make of this postmodern critique? We suggest that, it is not the business of postmodern inquiry to be politically committed or active, merely to observe and comment. In another but related critique, postmodernism by promoting introverted intrinsically gratifying contemplation may obstruct activism by inducing lethargy. This we suspect is why postmodernism has been called the 'opiate of the intelligentsia'. How do we break its meaning down in order to achieve results? We argue that it is not a difficult task just a different perspective is required to different tasks. However, we agree that there should be some misgivings with poststructuralist theory.

Critics working from within critical social theory frameworks have pointed to the shortcomings of poststructuralist theory and therefore the means of contributing to valuable knowledge. They question for example, the epistemological basis of its overall social strategy that is possible given that the notion of power does not, as Fraser (1989) indicates, given credence to notions of force, domination and legitimation. For it is claimed social change cannot come about when the notion of power is conceived without foundation, without a sense of what 'ought' to happen. Furthermore, the emphasis on language and textuality, proposed in poststructuralism, is argued not to have grounding in political action. In other words, the relational notion of power is seen to lack emancipatory intent, via either the dialectic between theory and practice, or communicative action. In other words, postmodernism understandings of power do not comply with normative frameworks of political practice.

Habermas warns that postmodernism fosters nihilism, relativism and political irresponsibility. He encourages us to remain true to the intentions of the Enlightenment, particularly to the belief in human reason to solve human problems. Yet, despite Habermas's feisty attempts to hold back the tides of irrationality—it is generally accepted that the credibility of critical theory has been severely dented by the advent of the postmodern project and because of this doubt attempts to rethink the movement are underway. As Ray and Rinzler (1993, pp ix) acknowledge, 'the notion of historically grounded reason, which offers both the legitimisation for critical theory and the impetus behind the resistance of oppression, has become unfashionable in an intellectual milieu informed by relativism and postmodernism.'

Making sense of postmodernism is thus a difficult task and one which has been carefully sidestepped by many sport managers and although we have tended to separate relativism and postmodernism as if they were mutually exclusive paradigms, the theories of the Frankfurt School and of poststructuralism do have some points of contact. In fact they have some contact in spite of some notable arguments between their major proponents. For a start, the theories are committed to the overthrow of our existing society and to the redesign, if not replacement, of some of its major institutions. Habermas for instance, is committed to a society where dominance and oppression are absent, where individuals are genuinely autonomous and not the tools of technical rationalism, where there is truthful exchange of ideas according to the principles of 'communicative competence'. Foucault on the other hand, places his faith in the fact that there is nothing essential about human nature or incorrigible about institutions. He suggests that just as modern society has crafted a particular type of human being and designed particular institutions to house them so some future society dominated by different imperatives could result in human beings and institutions having a rather different nature and character. The points of difference from both Habermas and Foucault thus centre on strategies for achieving human emancipation. Those following Habermas seem to place considerable faith in the capacity of individuals to overthrow technical rationality by confronting the state and setting an alternative social arrangement based on the humanist principles of liberty and justice, rationality and truth. Foucault's agenda is somewhat less ambitious and centres on intervening in local sites and on reforming them in the light of a more libertarian agenda if needs be, with an abandonment of the humanist inheritance.

We agree that certainly there is a pessimism permeating postmodernism which is not shared by the critical theorists. We have also argued that not only is there a wariness towards expressing any faith in the future or the possibility of constructive social action, but there is also a somewhat ritualistic attitude towards the past, which is heavily weighted in particular towards the Enlightenment project and humanism generally.

In concluding this section we argue that although these scholars present some good reasons to be skeptical of the relevance of postmodernism the fact remains that postmodernism provides a welcome challenge to the absolution of the modern era.

Characteristics of Postmodernism

Paramount in the postmodern shift is a re-examination of the values, beliefs, and practices perpetuated by elites that serve to suppress the expression of minority viewpoints. The importance of finding a single totalitarian truth or commonality is replaced by the realization that multiple truths exist simultaneously and that the real issue is not what the truth is but which one is being allowed to be heard. Therefore by focusing attention on social processes (e.g. power, control, conflict) operating below the surface of our awareness, postmodernism challenges the monopoly of currently dominant orthodoxies. Consequently, the context, content, and methods of entire disciplines have become more open than ever before to continuous rethinking, reanalysis and reinterpretation. Sport management has not heeded the warnings postulated by the postmodern phenomenon and there are many areas, which would benefit from an analysis of the perspective. The works of 'experts' prior to this book considered 'major' contributors are being examined for biases attributable to their membership in dominant groups. The view of critics deconstructing the grand narrative (modern assumptions of objectivism, positivism and reductionism) are being given increasing hearing and weight. In short, academia is witnessing an explosion of reflexivity, wherein its time-honoured institutions are being increasingly challenged for their relevance. Academics in the sport management area need to take more notice of the warnings from this section of the academic world and begin to experience the perspectives put forward by such scholars as Michel Foucault.

Postmodern ideas dispute both traditional disciplinary content and method. Indeed, they draw attention to the limitations of disciplinary content itself, opening the doors to the inclusion of alternative knowledge structures and interpretations. In other words, the relevant content domains of disciplines are not quite as singularly clear as before and are increasingly challenged as incomplete or inappropriate. Boundaries between adjoining disciplines are more loosely defined. Transboundary (interdisciplinary) work is considered the cutting edge of knowledge generation. Sport managers could do worse than consider other interrelated disciplines in order to enhance the knowledge base of the profession. However, as we all know research is characterized by a multiplicity of oftentimes conflicting theories, models, findings and interpretations each addressing a particular view of the phenomenon under study and each having limited relevance to the external world so that the contingencies around which theoretical tenets revolve are themselves increasingly contingent on other factors.

Disciplinary tenets, methods and claims previously shared in taken-for-granted ways by a relatively homogeneous faculty, and consensually communicated to students without question as to their veracity or applicability, are increasingly under attack for being the historical knowledge rather than a knowledge useful for underlying the profession. Furthermore, they are challenged for being based on no less arbitrary premises than any other set of explanations and prescriptions. Prominent discourse is drawing attention to the limiting nature of modern disciplinary content (i.e. feminist discourse). This is principally because disciplinary content domains are increasingly open to diverse interpretations and the inclusion of alternative representations questions the scope of what is legitimate and appropriate knowledge in the academic enterprise.

Moreover, postmodernism highlights the fundamental uncontrollability of our meanings about theory. The 'out there' is constructed by 'our discursive conceptions of it and these conceptions are collectively sustained and continually renegotiated in the process of making sense' (Parker, 1992, p. 3). Scientific research is praised for creating factual observations that are then recorded. There is a search for wholeness and interconnectedness rather than the fragmentation of the researched phenomena. In this form of research intuition, inner wisdom and ways of knowing that emphasize inner authority; integrity and personal reflection are accentuated rather than reliance on rational analysis and externalization of reality and authority. Modern methods of scientific examination and expert-driven discourse are supplanted by postmodern methods of conversation that allow the emergence of multiple realities and the realization of the limitations of currently dominant paradigms. Thus making the research stronger, more rounded and thorough.

Postmodernism and Sport Management

The major appeal of postmodernism for sport management researchers is the rejection of scientific objectivity and the celebration of the value of differing discourses and appealing philosophy of an occupation whose knowledge base and practices have traditionally been viewed as a poor relation to both management and marketing.

The challenges of postmodernist influences on sport management academics appear to be:

- A rejection of positivism as a foundation for knowledge because of its tendency to ignore the fact that 'objectivity' is just as constructed and provisional as 'subjectivity'.
- Rejection of sport management models and metaparadigms. Postmodernism encourages the co-existence, juxtaposition and interaction of multiple paradigms.
- To break down categorisations of phenomena to avoid hegemonic forms of knowledge.
- To emphasize the importance of multiple, relativistic constructions of reality, and the ambiguity and complexity in everyday life as a sport manager.

- To focus attention on social processes (e.g. power, control, conflict) operating below the surface of our awareness so as to challenge the monopoly of currently dominant orthodoxies.

- To emphasis interpretative research methodologies which allow multiple explanations for the phenomena of concern to sport management.

- To facilitate and allow sport managers to tell their own stories and clarify their own issues in order to find their own solutions. This leads to the local development of texts, techniques and practices.

- To re-examine the values, beliefs and practices perpetuated by 'experts' that serve to dominate sport management discourse—the real issue is not what the truth is but which one is being heard.

- To identify and critically examine the discourses, practices and relationships of our practice worlds in order to determine the extent to which they encompass hidden elements of power and domination.

- To examine understandings of how sport management practice itself, may have been and be, stopped by social, economic and political factors that are external to the art of sport management itself.

- To include the 'voices' of all who are affected in sport management.

- Ultimately, to empower sport management practitioners to take control of their destiny.

Applying Postmodernism to Sport Management Theory

Postmodern analysis can illuminate the techniques used by sport management to legitimate its own knowledge claims and the various often-competing discourses embedded in sport management discourse. They can reveal the nature of the interplay between sport management 'experts' and practitioners. For example, in sport management research the technocratic discourse operates in such a way as to limit the sport manager's perception of practice. In this manner, the power afforded to the technocratic/managerial discursive framework is such that it is very difficult for sport management practitioners to move away from a traditional management approach to become a more reflective practitioner as they become constrained by the demands of their position.

A recent analysis of popular sport management textbooks provides an example of the constraining influence of dominant discursive frameworks on sport management. Based upon the authors readings of these texts it would appear that there is a serious disjuncture between the managerial world presented in the texts and the actual world of sport management practice. Interestingly, the textbooks analysed indicated the use of power and its structures to maintain a technical approach to behaviour in sport management. Thereby highlighting the schematization of sport management.

Whilst this management approach is important and of course has a part to play in sport management practice the effect of this discourse in these textbooks leads to the exclusion of other equally important and valid discourses which are integral to the development of the reflective sport manager. Instead, sport management discourse as it is portrayed in these texts provides 'rules' and 'receipts' on which to base sport management practice. The development of such objective sport management 'truth' is such that it is difficult for sport managers to conceptualise any other basis for practice. However, the analysis of sport management knowledge informed by a postmodern perspective, offers further potential for power relations, which frame sport management knowledge, to be displaced.

Several Postmodern questions that would challenge the conditions of existence of the discourse of sport management theory, for example, could include the following. What types of practices or discussions had to be in place before the discourse of sport management could be constructed? What social practices and power arrangements are necessary for the discourse of sport management theory to continue? What implicit rules are there in the discourse of sport management theory that assists to validate its existence? What is the relationship between theory and practice in the discourse of sport management? If these and other questions were taken up by academics we could open a new forum for debate and discussion that could only enhance and promote the knowledge base and ultimately enhance the profession.

It is argued that sport management research must however, move beyond pre-occupation with questioning and produce explanatory and predictive principles from the interpretation. In this way we argue in this book that he consequences of postmodern analysis of sport managements' theoretical basis should be that:

1.   Theory is demystified. What is called sport management theory is viewed as an elaboration of day-to-day thinking and reflection.
2.   Theory is seen as a way of seeing and apprehending the world, a prescription for perception, a pair of epistemological spectacles through which the world is seen in various and different ways.
3.   Theory is examined in a historical, social, economic, cultural and political context.
4.   Theory is acknowledged as a regime of truth, these regimes being part and parcel of a research culture that has well defined characteristics.

The potential contribution of a postmodern critique in this way would address such notions as the 'taken-for-grantedness' of specific sport management practices, the history of sport management practices, power relations within specific sport management discourses, the vested interests of participants and their authorised voice.

Examples of sport management issues that would possibly benefit from postmodern critique include examining the discourses of power, professionalism, practice, policy, gender, racism and culture to name just a few. Analyses in areas such as the above could only assist and contribute to the development of sport management as an academic discipline. We strongly stipulate that without such analysis the profession cannot more towards having a truly reflective approach to its future and will remain a Cinderella profession out of the mainstream management arena.

Implications for Sport Management Research

There is little doubt that speaking 'with the confidence of standing at the cutting edge of time and of being able to speak for others' (Huyssen, 1990, p. 271) is no longer an option in a postmodern intellectual climate. Instead, we are being challenged to move from the universal, the time honoured and the infallible to the tentative and the precarious. The postmodern sport management researcher must wade into unchartered territory for which there are no blueprints. All blueprints as 'grand narrative' are definitely viewed as doubtful. This situation is laudable for scholarship but lamented by those who want security. Security we feel can no longer be an option in the current university research milieu. Indeed, we must take risks and branch out into the unknown and lead the field into uncharted waters through the experimentation and delivery of new theory that both informs and drives the profession.

It is therefore more than tempting to spend our energies mourning the passing of the good old days. Or more comforting still, we could ignore the imperatives of contemporary social theorising and continue to make forays up abandoned intellectual gullies. Indeed, it would be more lucrative and less troublesome to do so. Breaking with certainty is daunting and demanding for researchers, when we transcend the anti-positivist, anti-empirical impetus that has characterised modernism in the past (Hebdudgem, 1988) we engage in research that is more challenging more controversial and more disturbing across ideological boundaries but filled with tension and uncertainty. We then push the boundaries of research and enhance our own thinking in ways in which we previously could not have imagined.

A final and arguably the most fundamental implication of postmodernism is the unavoidable process of critical self-appraisal that it imposes on the sport management field. Postmodernism in sum compels sport management researchers and practitioners to examine theoretical accomplishments, question their epistemological assumptions and continually approve and improve the appropriateness of their methodological procedures.

The following principles are a response to the methodological concerns raised in postmodern inquiry.

- Acknowledgment is made of the researchers' values, interests, interactions and interpretations within the research process.
- Acknowledgment is made of the reasons for undertaking research.
- Research is regarded as a mutually participative, creative process, wherein the 'voice' of the participants is valued and recognised in the research process.
- Acknowledgment is made of the authorial self as intrusive, but as indispensable to the research process.
- Encouragement is given to facilitate and allow individuals to tell their own stories, to identify their own issues and find their own solutions beyond the activities of the researcher.

There are benefits for both practitioner and researcher in exploring existing postmodern debates to sharpen their own critical consciousness. The researcher will increasingly identify dimensions of the reflexive nature of researcher and participant intersubjectivity and the reflexive moments of research interaction. Because of their vantage point in interacting intensively at multiple levels and in an enduring way with people from all walks of life sport managers are well positioned to take up many of the challenges of postmodern critique. By doing so they can integrate these challenges into the orthodoxy of current research methods and in their application in the field.

Despite the strong support for adopting a postmodern approach to research Parson (1994) identifies limitations of postmodernism applied to research. She claims that postmodernist researchers have surrendered reliability and 'bathed in the glow of detailed and accurate accounts of their research participants' lives' resulting in '...the absence of a true (valid) base upon which to construct social theory' (p. 23). She identified this as the 'crisis of legitimation'. She identifies a second crisis arising from the application of postmodernism to research as the 'crisis of representation'. This relates to the problems of defending representations of research participants as legitimate rather than merely as constructions of the researcher. This is a particular problem for research approaches that deliberately set out to take participants' stories through increasing levels of abstraction. Consequently, we need to be aware that postmodernism is not a panacea which solves all of our problems but a set of theories which if utilized correctly can only further enhance knowledge.

Concluding Comments

It may be that the authors have begun to convince some readers thinking about the possibility of postmodern research to abandon work, hope, or both. This has not been our intention. The type of academic who ought to be informing sport management thought in the current intellectual climate is one who is unintimidated by rarefied debate. As Featherstone (1991, p. 13) so eloquently demonstrated, 'anyone who considers postmodernism a passing fancy will do so at considerable peril to oneself and needs to examine one's intellectual position before it is too late'. It is important that potentially transformative sport management research be forthcoming to challenge traditional practices.

In endeavouring to emulate rigorous standards of research sport management research has frequently down played and de-emphasized the creativity, spontaneity and individual insight that often characterised successful sport management practices. Firat (1992) indicates that 'postmodernism gives all of us an opportunity to be honest with ourselves to discard our pretences and to climb down from our pedestals and be both self-critical and celebratory'.

This means among other things, more experimentation across disciplines and paradigms, more methodological 'risks', more eclectic research approaches. In a practical sense and by implication, it means journal reviewers who are open to the possibility of new forms of research writing. This situation we feel is long overdue and should be addressed without delay.

The implications for research are that there should be an increase in postmodern research in sport management and research forms could range from postmodern ethnographies, life histories, narratives, story telling to visual and symbolic representation. Moreover, as sport management academics become more familiar with postmodern thought they should ask social, political and professional questions about what is 'taken for granted' in sport management discourse, and how things evolved to create the current situation. Although, relatively few sport managers may undertake such analyses and that postmodernism may remain in the short term at the fringes of sport management research the publication of such work will change the perspectives of sport management academics. What is also certain is that academics in sport management cannot ignore the changes occurring in other fields such as philosophy, sociology, and the core discipline of management. In short if we continue to ignore other theory we will be responsible for our own demise. Is this the legacy, which we wish to leave the profession?

Chapter 3

Towards Critical Theory in Sport Management

...intellectuals should maintain a critical attitude toward their work: they should examine and make explicit its relationship to the current state of society and socially created knowledge.

Wallace & Wolf (1986: 98)

What is Critical Theory?

Critical theory is both a philosophical position and a process of theorising, and more importantly, it is a process grounded in an explicit philosophical position. Despite its apparent pessimistic grounding in radical critiques of society, we believe that critical theory should be seen as a profoundly optimistic theory. In our opinion this optimism arises from its promise to provide sport management researchers with possibilities for transforming existing social orders in ways that reflect conditions of freedom, equality and justice.

A precise definition of critical theory is therefore elusive. The critical theory approach strives both to understand and reveal the workings of the broad political, economic, social and cultural processes, and to explore the inner sanctums of human consciousness where the meanings of social life are constructed. This is in contrast to traditional theories, which claim to be objective and neutral, and critical theory is manifestly political, within a priori commitment to take sides with the oppressed and those whose interests are contravened by external sources of domination. Critical theorists flatly reject any notion that theory should guide practice, seeing this as yet another form of domination. Instead, change comes about as one's awareness of the limitation and constraints upon human potential are clearly perceived.

The above brief sketch of critical theory belies the sophistication and complexity of the analysis of the individual and society developed by critical theorists over the last few decades. In order to grasp a greater understanding of the central themes of critical theory it is necessary to visit its origins.

The Origins of Critical Theory

Critical theory dates back to Socrates upholding the reality of ideas or forms over the reality of appearances. Over the millennia this debate on interpretation and representation became the intellectual foundation of philosophy, communications and education. More recently the origins of critical theory are found in Kant's *Critique of Pure Reason*, published in 1781, and in the tradition of German idealism that followed. Critical theory in its modern forms evolved during the 1920s and 1930s and all but faded into obscurity during the 1940s, and then resurfaced in the post-war era. In recent years, critical theory has been the focus of much interest and controversy in academic circles around the world. The scope of critical theory encompasses the realms of social philosophy, theory and practice, and embraces substantive concerns ranging from economic system to psychology. Rather than being a totally unified perspective, the tenets of critical theory come to us in several schools of thought, notably via Gramsci in Italy, Lukacs in Hungary, and especially through the work of a group of German scholars collectively known as the Frankfurt School. Prominent among this group were Max Horkheimer, Theodore Adorno, and Herbert Marase. The work of Jurgen Habermas, though removed in time for the early Frankfurt School also stems from this tradition.

The Frankfurt School, and the so-called critical theory which stemmed from it, explores the human condition from a similar starting point. With a renewed focus upon the problem of the individual, the Frankfurt School was also oriented towards Freudian psychoanalysis, interpreting the problems of neuroses, and psychopathologies in general, in terms of the failure of a capitalist society to allow the individual free rein and autonomous expression. In effect, the Frankfurt School updated Marxism, preserving its belief that all problems to do with society stemmed from the economic sphere, but adding to it the plight of a society shackled to the debilitating effects of technical rationality and an efficient division of labour. In effect, it is these factors, which have provided capitalism with tools of economic and material success, but at the expense of a genuinely democratic society in which all individuals can participate and find themselves fulfilled. The Frankfurt School is particularly committed to a view of the social sciences that emphasises a comprehensive critique of existing social arrangements.

The Frankfurt School's criticism of knowledge of truth claims were cast in a broad context within a subjectivist perspective, as Held (1980) describes:

> Each of the critical theorists maintained that although all knowledge is historically conditioned, truth claims could be rationally adjudicated independently of immediate social (i.e. class) interests. They defended the possibility of an independent moment of criticism. They also all attempted to justify critical theory on a non-objectivistic and materialistic foundation. The extension and development of the notion of critique, from a concern with the conditions and limits of reason of knowledge (Kant), to a reflection on the emergence of spirit (Hegel), and then to a focus on specific historical forms-capitalism, the exchange process (Marx)—was furthered in the work of the Frankfurt theorists and Habermas. They sought to develop a critical perspective in the discussion of all social practices. (pp. 15–16)

In summary several features of the Frankfurt School critical theory are noteworthy. These are that:

1. Much of the impetus for the development of critical theory came from the problems of positivism as it gained wide currency in the social sciences.
2. Unlike classical Marxism with its stress on economic determinism, critical theory stresses the importance and possibility of individual action.
3. A major focus for critical theory is the critique of technical rationality and its preoccupation with efficiency, instrumentality and means over ends. The anti-positivist stance which is characteristic of the theory derives not so much from being anti-science, but from a recognition that modern-day science has lost its connection with politics and ethics, which checks the excesses of positivism. In this critique, technical rationality is regarded as the dominant force in the modern world and as one, which must be challenged in the name of emancipation.
4. The study of culture is central to critical theory, for culture provides a focus for understanding and shaping the possibilities of autonomy and independence from technical and practical interests. In particular, critical theory is drawn to the domain of aesthetics because of its capacity to transcend the economic sphere and to produce oppositional forms of cultural production.

However, the form of critical theory developed by the Frankfurt School of the 1930s is justifiably criticised by Habermas, as pertaining to hybrid German philosophical traditions. Viewing the Frankfurt School's critical theory as restrictively rooted in the polarised politics of past decades, Habermas sought to move critical theory beyond the Frankfurt School and continue the project of 'enlightenment' in order to complete the project of modernity.

Habermas and Critical Theory

Jurgen Habermas, the major heir of the Frankfurt School philosophy, developed an exposition of the 'interests' which not only make culture and society possible but also directs our research for knowledge: 'technical' interest, 'practical' interest and 'emancipatory' interest. The scope of his work is immense ranging from political polemics to intensely theoretical discourses on hermeneutics, and it is still in progress. Through all his work Habermas reflects the characteristic distrust critical theory has for positivism or scientism. He regards the growth of science, technology and bureaucratisation as combining state power and capitalist control in a way that provokes crisis. A crisis of legitimation (stemming from the impotence of 'authorities'): a crisis a motivation (stemming from the powerlessness of the individual): and a crisis of identity (stemming from a lack of sense of collective identity).

Through his critique of late capitalism Habermas goes beyond Marx's analysis of the crisis tendencies of 'classical' capitalism. Habermas identifies one aspect of contemporary culture as its reliance on the technocratic/bureaucratic expert who thrives on efficiency, which derives from the technique's relentless quest for a controlled environment. All this in close alliance with what is perceived as marketplace imperatives and of technology's peculiar view of rationality and effectiveness, of progress and even of meaning. Habermas calls this form of rationality 'instrumental rationality'. He argues that the all-pervasive inner logic of instrumental rationality has begun to take over other areas of human culture. The criterion of instrumentality is applied to more and more relationships, replacing reflective or communicative modes as the dominant mode of human interaction with the world. Instrumentality derives from the 'technical interest', which is evidence of the basic human need to control and manage the environment. According to the Habermasian critique, this cultural change has transformed human institutions. In particular, it has provoked a crisis in politics, a crisis for the state so that the scope of politics becomes basically reduced to a question of who can run the economy best—a matter of technical decision-making.

Sport management, has become enmeshed in this crisis and is now an object of this same pragmatic, technical decision-making, a prisoner of technocratic values. These values are also the values of the marketplace and managerialism: competition, efficiency, utility, performance indicators, practicability and profitability.

In his more recent work Habermas' methodological approach is derived from his 'theory of social evolution'. This is abstract and complex, but can be understood by reference of three key interrelated variables. These are what he calls a 'life-world', 'systems' and 'language decentration' (cf. Giddens, 1979; Habermas, 1981a/1984; Habermas, 1981b/1987). The life-world is to Habermas, a type of cultural space that gives meaning and nature to societal life. Whilst separate and distinct from the more tangible (technical) visible 'system' it is the social reality, which gives these systems meaning and attempts to guide their behaviour through 'steering mechanisms'. Systems are the 'self-regulating action contexts which co-ordinate actions around specific mechanisms or media, such as money or power' (Thompson, 1983, p. 285). They are, in this sense, distinct elements whilst at the same time intended to be the tangible expression of the cultural life-world. Language decentration traces the way individuals develop their language skills that to Habermas enable the differentiation of the life-world and systems and the development of both.

Habermas separates two historical learning processes and forms of rationality. He argues for the systematic improvement of the life-world through as expanded conception of rationality focusing on the creation and re-creation of patterns of meaning. The life-world can be regarded as fully rational, rather than instrumentalized or strategized, to the extent that it permits interactions that are guided by communicatively achieved understanding rather than by imperatives from the system world. Communicatively achieved understanding is dependent on undistorted communication, the presence of free discussion based on goodwill, argumentation and dialogue. On the basis of undistorted rational discussion he assumes that consensus can be reached regarding both present and desirable states. Undistorted communication provides the basis for the 'highest' form of rationality, namely communicative rationality. However, communicative rationality denotes a way of responding to (questioning, testing and possibly accepting) the validity of different claims. Finally, communicative action thus allows for the exploration of every statement on a basis of the following (universal) validity criteria: comprehensibility, sincerity, truthfulness and legitimacy. Communicative action is therefore an important aspect of social interaction in society, in social institutions and in daily life. The ideal speech situation, which enables communicative rationality and is in turn pervaded by it, exists under the following conditions. 'The structure of communication itself produces no constraints if and only if, for all possible participants, there is a symmetrical distribution of chances to choose and to apply speech-act' (Habermas, cited by Hesse 1982, p. 113).

> The impact of the work of Habermas has been felt both directly and indirectly by sport management theorists. Critical theory recognises than an emancipated society is one in which human beings actively control their own destinies, through a heightened understanding of the circumstances in which they live. Furthermore, critical theory encourages self-criticism and continuing critique through a praxis method, which implies emancipation from ideological dogmatism and the transformation of authoritarian systems through democratic communication processes. Central to this is the critique of domination and the ways those subjugated actively participate is their own subjugation.

The End of Critical Theory?

Over the years Habermas has raised the stakes for critical theorizing and has brought its fundamental epistemological problem into the open; the paradox of self-grounding. In order to be 'critical' such theories must be relatively external to the ideas and institutions which currently prevail; they cannot share too much of the conceptual framework of the objects of critique in order to count as 'critical'. But equally critical theory cannot entirely sever its links to this framework since it emerges as its radical self-reflection. For Horkheimer and Adorno the 'framework' in question was the enlightenment tradition. Critical theorizing must also attach itself imminently to ideas and institutions in order to express a 'not-yet-realized' and counterfactual potential within them, otherwise it remains merely utopian. It is this dialectical tension between the possible and the actual, between validity and facticity, which lies at the heart of all political theorizing but which is particularly acute for critical theory. Connerton (1980) expressed the difficulty for critical theory in terms of its need to appeal to, and on behalf of a 'critical public sphere, which is never firmly localized' (p.137).

Critical theory has always been self-conscious of its status as mere argument, of certain remoteness from the practices on the 'far side of discourse.' As Habermas has developed and refined the theory of communicative action, his status as a critical theorist in its classic sense has become more problematic, especially as the grounding process appealed to abstract communicative principles.

Hoy and McCarthy (1994) took a sustained critique of the Habermasian project. Their point of departure is two questions: What is 'critical' about critical theory? And must one have a 'theory' in order to be critical? Against Habermas, they argued that universalism contributes nothing whatsoever to the 'critical' force of critical theory. Relatedly, they are highly sceptical of the idea that criticism needs theory at all. For Hoy and McCarthy, Habermas's universal pragmatics (critical theory) comes out much the worse for its encounter with Foucault's genealogy (critical history). Similar objections are marshalled from a hermeneutic perspective against the abstract theoreticism and homogenizing universalism of Habermas's project.

Whereas the primary concern of Hoy and McCarthy (1994) was to initiate an academic debate, Bronner's (1994) aim was to save critical theory from academic normalization. His work is a forceful reminder that traditional theorists have only interpreted the world, but the point for the critical theorist is to change it.

Critical Theory in Organisation and Management Research

Researchers in organization and management studies came to critical theory writings relatively late, with critical theory emerging in the late 1970s and 1980s (i.e. Benson, 1977; Burrell and Morgan, 1979; Frost, 1980; Deetz and Kersten, 1983; Fischer and Sirianni, 1984). Part of the reason critical theory has now found fertile ground in management studies is the decline and disillusionment of what is broadly referred to as modernist assumptions by both organizational theorists and practitioners.

Modernism is exemplified in the field of management and organization studies by the embrace of Taylorism, Fordism and more recently in the technologies of flexible specialisation. Modernist organisations may be thought of in terms of Max Weber's (1978) typification of bureaucracy. Its key processes were signified by a modernising project composed of tendencies. These include, an increasing specialization; hierarchization; stratification; normalization; standardization and centralization of organizational action.

Management as a modernist discourse works on the basis of control, the progressive rationalization and colonization of nature and people, whether workers, potential consumers, or society as a whole. But there are structural limits to control. The shift from manufacturing to service industries as the mast typical economic form in the western world has had implications for control forms. Objectives for management control are decreasing labour power and behaviour and increasing the mind power and subjectivities of employees. These new social conditions provide a new urgency and new areas of application for critical theory work in organisation studies (for overviews see Alvesson, 1993a; Willmott, 1993). These indicate the new social conditions to which critical theory have provided innovative and instructive analyses. The central goal of critical theory in organizational and management studies has been to create societies and workplaces which are free from domination, where all members have an equal opportunity to contribute to the production of systems which meet human needs and lead to the progressive development of all. Critical theorists sometimes have a clear political agenda focused on the interests of specific identifiable groups such as women, workers or people of colour, but usually address general issues of goals, values, forms of consciousness and communicative distortions within corporations. Increasingly important to critical studies is the enrichment of the knowledge base, improvement of decision process and increases in 'learning' and adaptation. In the context of management and organisation studies it should be emphasised that critical theory is not anti-management even though it tends to treat management as institutionalised and ideologies and practices of management as expressions of contemporary forms of domination.

Alvession and Willmott (1996) have pointed at some metaphors for organizations and management from critical theory: organization as technocracy; mystification; cultural doping; and colonizing power. These draw attention to how management expertise leads to passivity on the part of other organizational participants, how ambiguity and contradictions are masked, how the engineering of values and definitions of reality tend to weaken low-level and other marginal groups in the negotiation of workplace reality. And respectively, how the codes of money and formal power exercise a close to hegemonic position over workplace experiences and articulated values and priorities.

The promises of critical theory that are either implied or made explicit relate to the nature of critical theory as a philosophical position and as a process of theorizing. There is a liberatory intent in using radical critiques to transform the existing restrictive social order and conditions within the status quo into those that are based and enacted on the principles of equality, freedom and justice. The emancipatory critique of critical theory relies on systematic reflection and promises freedom from the distorted understandings communication and activities of pre-existing social structures, giving possibilities for new ways of being and acting within them.

Critical theory then, in its concern with the ways in which human being are not only shaped by the circumstances of their own existence but actually shape them promises to move us beyond a socio-historical determinism. This move is away from the reification of social constructions, away from the portrayal of existing social orders relationships and practices as 'natural', 'inevitable' and 'immutable'—the only 'logical' way of ordering our existence. Critical theorists alert us to the notion that knowledge and forms of social existence are constructed by 'human beings' and hence they become interested, that is they serve particular identifiable human interest (Habermas, 1971). They also alert us to the possibility that the very means of interpretation and communication may be dominated by particular groupings in a given social order. As such the interests of dominant groupings may be maintained at the expense of the interests of others not only by direct coercion but also by the force of intellectual and moral leadership. Providing the basis by which people may come to reclaim the power to interpret and give meaning to, and hence to structure their social existence is perhaps the most important offering of critical theory.

Critical theory exposes to us our power to shape rather than simply be shaped by our social forms of existence. It is concerned with exploring the tension between the given (what exists or what we understand to exist) and the possible, that is between the ways in which our 'lifeworlds' are presently constructed and the ways that they could be constructed. Critical theorising then promises us the opportunity to come to a cognitive understanding of our worlds particularly our social existence, and in so doing move beyond the dominant social order to reconstruct our worlds in just and liberating ways.

Given these promises, what claims might then be made with regard to the offerings of critical theory for sport management?

Critical Theory and Sport Management

In sport management we have engaged in self-examination, introspection and most often self-criticism. We have looked to find ways in which we might gain 'improved standards of practice' and we have largely treated questions of practice as technical questions to be answered empirically. Improvements have been seen to lie in manipulation of various factors within the institution of sport management itself, factors such as sport management education and practice.

Within sport management we have extolled the virtues of solid research and formal theoretical base. We have developed expertise in research, education and administration and have begun to talk about, although seldom acknowledged or identified in any real way, expert sport management practice. We have also given little attention to questions of explanation. That is—what is it that we are really doing as sport managers? Why is it that others and we act in the ways that we do? How did the state of affairs that we experience come to exist? Are there other possibilities in the ways that we can understand and act in our worlds?

Much of this is symptomatic of the dominant technical rationality that pervades our existence. Such rationality is not itself questioned, nor is the practices and relationships that such rationality perpetuates, and by which it is maintained. Although many of us have begun to find virtue in political awareness we have largely limited our concerns to technical manipulation of and within existing structures without addressing in any real way the legitimacy of these structures and relationships.

We hear sport managers talk about professionalisation, the control of practice the development of a distinct body of knowledge and so on. Indeed, we have identified professionalisation, autonomy and control of practice as perhaps the key issues facing us today. Yet in relation to the discourse of professionalisation in sport management, change is generally seen as needing to occur within sport management itself, in isolation from any real consideration of wider institutional structures.

Critical theory encourages us to focus on sport management as a personally and socially constructed activity. We are asked to examine our understandings of and in the institution of sport management in terms of the ways in which such understandings, and hence practice itself, may have been, and be, shaped by social and political factors that are external to the act of sport management itself. Critical theory asks us to identify and critically examine the discourses, practices and relationships of our practice worlds in order to determine the extent to which they encompass hidden elements of power and domination that fail to serve interests that we would wish to acknowledge as legitimate.

Critical theory also claims to promise us the possibility of coming to understand our worlds in an empowering way. Critical theory therefore offers us the challenge of reconstructing our social worlds in ways that are less distorted by relations of power and domination, of finding for ourselves new, less oppressive more just ways of structuring our existence. As sport managers, we can begin to critically engage in critical examinations of our worlds by asking such questions as:

- To what extent does what we 'know' personally of and believe about our sport management worlds reflective of the ways we would wish to conceive our practice?
- To what extent are our actions shaped by forces external to ourselves and to sport management?
- To what extent are our sport management understandings beliefs, experiences and practices contradictory?
- To what extent is what we believe (or say we believe or would wish to believe) about practice supported by present institutional structures and relationships?
- Whose interests do the present state of affairs serve? How did it come to be this way? How is it perpetuated? In what way do we ourselves contribute to the maintenance of the status quo?
- What are the natures of the discourses that we presently engage in? To what extent are these discourses politicised and to what extent do they simply serve to mystify and maintain existing unjust relations of power and domination?
- What other possibilities are there for us in the reconstruction of our sport management worlds?

Critical theory promises us (sport researchers and managers) the possibility of subjecting existing social orders to critical scrutiny and provides us with some of the conceptual tools to do so. Sport management itself is a social construction not an object, it is shaped by people who bring to it their own understandings of the world. It is not something that exists external to people and their interactions with one another. As a consequence of acknowledging this it becomes clear that we should consistently subject to critical scrutiny our understandings and actions as sport managers, and the ways in which we shape and are shaped by our worlds. We need to subject to scrutiny our practices and relationships, noting particularly the interests that are served by maintaining the status quo.

Individuals in sport management must come to accept an ongoing evolution or even revolution in our understandings and practice of sport management both at personal and collective levels. In our ongoing search we should seek to expose, understand and overcome the contradictions and frustrations that we and others experience. In so doing critical theory has the opportunity to influence sport management praxis. The concept of praxis has been introduced into literature largely since 1970 when Freire's *Pedagogy of the Oppressed* was published in English. Freire (1972) was using praxis to refer to 'reflection and action upon the world in order to transform it' (p. 28). Thus, in the process of liberation praxis becomes central in the dialectical relationship between thought and action. This distinguishes theory for its own sake on the one hand and pure action or activism on the other.

In sport management research a critical praxis can facilitate freedom for sport managers to question what is knowledge, how we know and who provides the evidence. Habermas (1971) contended that critical theory helps to uncover what ought to be done in order to create and to support self-reflection. Without critical reflection patterns of communication and socialization are reproduced and inevitably determine the theoretical and research traditions that are perpetuated without being challenged.

By analysing how and why embedded assumptions guide theory development, research and practice sport managers can begin to describe and explain oppressive effects. Habermas (1981a/1984) contended that researchers have a responsibility to identify constraining circumstances in society and to assist in liberation from oppressive structures. Determination can be made as to whether goals can be achieved through critical praxis and self-reflection. The process of critical reflection is praxis, because the ends and the means are directed toward transformation. Critical approaches promise us the possibility of examining our sport management worlds in terms of moral and political as well as simply technical concerns. In accepting the political interested nature of our activities we are provided with the conceptual tools to theorise our practice and to reconstruct it. Such theorising is long overdue.

It would be accurate to suggest that critical theory has not been a dominant mode of research in sport management. However, the impact of critical theory is increasing and critical theory research (Chalip, 1996) has recently appeared in sport management journals. It would appear that critical theory is a fertile ground for sport management research and should be continued.

Critical Sport Management Research

Researchers exploring the possibilities of research located within critical theory perspectives generally take the view that the interpretations, values and interests of the participants are central to the research process. Truths are grasped not by eliminating subjectivity, but through the intersubjectivity of subject and object, as meaning through dialogue emerges. In this way participants and researchers are recognized as part of the social world that they study. The researcher may take a facilitative role, allowing the participants to define the research problem or alternatively, develop a research design that acknowledges an intimate relationship between the researcher and participants.

Participative and collaborative research designs, such as action research and critical ethnography are seen to allow an empowering and emanicipatory role for research. As a consequence of the prevailing division of intellectual labour, the critical project is principally the responsibility of the academic section of the sport management profession. Critical researchers are being called upon to add a crucial dimension to their traditional knowledge base and teaching functions. By extending their research activities to include critical theory, sport management academics may be brought into more direct contact with their colleagues in practice. This should enable them to establish whether sport management is a profession whose members commonly have access to opportunities to exercise a considerable degree of power and influence, or, as is possibly the case, a profession in which most individuals are simply doing a job under conditions over which they have little or no control.

Importantly, It will also allow critical sport management researchers to learn of the reservations which their colleagues in practice have about the work they are involved in and the particular aspects of their professional lives which they find the most distressing or oppressive.

For the critical sport management researcher, impact on practice is an issue to be addressed throughout the research rather than after the study is completed. Therefore, for the critical theory paradigm the question is not 'does research affect practice' but 'does this research empower participants to change their lives'? The primary focus is on impact in the specific setting in which the research was conducted. However, critical theorists do choose to publish their work with the intention that it has a broader impact. The hope is not that the results can be directly applied in other settings but that reading the study will inspire others to critically examine their own circumstances. The research dissemination process seeks to provide 'consciousness-raising' experiences for the reader.

Forester's (1993) work combines theoretical sophistication with an empirical and applied orientation and can serve as an example here of what critical can look like in practice. To Forester, an empirically oriented critical theory should comprise of three components and be: '(1) empirically sound and descriptively meaningful; (2) interpretatively plausible and phenomenologically meaningful; and yet (3) critically pitched and ethically insightful' (p. 2).

Concluding Comments

While critical theory undoubtedly has much to offer sport management there are certainly a number of potential traps that we should take care to avoid. Critical theorists often claim that critique of existing social formations may in principle occur unhindered by ideological constrains such as those that it seeks to identify and overcome. However, critical theory has not as yet, provided a fully adequate account of opposing social movements and of differing interpretations of needs and interests. The interests and meanings that we identify for ourselves as sport managers and for sport management may contradict with those that others would wish to propose; and there may be no simple resolution to such disagreements, divisions and conflicts.

Another trap that we may fall into is that of believing that in surfacing elements we will be able to automatically to reconstruct our social worlds, resist domination and no longer participate in maintaining the conditions of our own domination or of the domination of others.

There is also a danger for sport management that in taking on the critical approaches uncritically we may expect more than might be reasonably offered. The notion that enlightenment will allow us to choose other forms of existence that are less repressive may not be borne out in our everyday experience, nevertheless, the most important phase of reconstruction of our individual and shared understandings by which we are at least alerted to the possibility that other forms of existence are possible. What this chapter is arguing is not that critical theory has nothing to offer sport management, but that in order to be consistent with a critical stance we must hold our critical theories critically. The dangers as already stated lie not in critical theory itself but in a naive acceptance and understanding of what critical theory may offer us. Clearly, unless we are to fall into the trap of dominating by defining the worlds of others for them, then it is essential that they not construct a new elite, or perpetuate ones that may already exist. A great deal of the direction and processes of change must come from the 'grassroots' levels in sport management not from an 'elite' who purport to know the interests of others. To know the contradictions that exist in a particular life form, to know the ways in which interests are constrained and denied in the process of domination by others, and to know the ways in which a form of existence can and should be transformed. Following on from a critical stance, change can only happen dialogically—dialogue that exposes the nature of our forms of existence, dialogue that exposes new possibilities and dialogues that exposes processes of change. There are not oracles to which we should, or can, turn for all the answers. In conclusion, critical approaches encourage us to constantly challenge our own understandings and assumptions about sport management in all aspects of our research including our practice as sport managers. Ultimately, the test of what critical theory really does offer us can only come as we engage in critical dialogue with each other and with our practice worlds. This is both the promise and the challenge of critical theory. The test of its success lies in the extent to which we find it useful in theorising the concerns, the struggles and the prospects of future sport management research.

Chapter 4

Deconstruction: A Strategy
for Inquiry

All in all, humanism and all it stands for has become a dirty word.

Plummer (2001: 256)

What is Deconstruction?

This chapter introduces a philosophical praxis termed deconstruction (Derrida, 1976, 1978, 1979, 1982, 1983, 1986, 1987) as one moment of the turn toward critical research. Deconstruction challenges an author's attempt to privilege a theory, technique or model as a superior way to arrive at closure around knowledge. Along with the critical historical practice of Michel Foucault, deconstruction challenges efforts to reduce the complexity of human existence to systems of explication, systems orchestrated by the author's theories, values and presuppositions.

Deconstruction shares with Foucauldian scholarship a desire to question Enlightenment models of rationality, theory, facticity and history as progress. This critical stance is perhaps best described by the intellectual movement termed postmodernism (see Lyotard, 1984), and attempt to arrive at a 'new beginning' for understanding the nature of human inquiry. As mentioned previously Postmodernism takes seriously the intellectual position that any metascheme for the production of knowledge can neither ground itself in anything other than an act of faith nor can it establish its capacity to insure that its own program can solve more problems than it creates. That knowledge in the human sciences is problematic arises from awareness that the powers of Enlightenment rationality, which were originally turned to mastery of nature, have now been turned to the mastery of human beings by other human beings. In other words the production of knowledge is never separable from the exercise of power (Foucault, 1980).

The challenge of deconstructionism is that it locates its understanding within a language game of textual analysis but presents its case as discovering multiple interpretations within texts (signifiers) which challenge meaning and identity. As no one interpretation is considered dominant or superior than another, deconstructionism is more a form of critique than of conclusive analysis.

Deconstructionism seeks to extrapolate signs and significations from a text, which operate within written texts but conform to language as their regulated function (Derrida, 1976). In this language game, the text acts as a signifier in which language becomes a chain of 'significations' and the author is seen as 'inscribed' within the text. Basically, this implies that multiple interpretations of text are valid and that, 'il n'y a pas hors-texte' (Derrida, 1976, p. 158)—'there is nothing outside the text'.

Derridian deconstructionism challenges notions of meaning and identity but does not advocate arbitrary interpretation. It is not anarchy in which any text can mean anything, nor is it the reproduction of emptiness where all texts are deconstructed into nothing.

> That person would have understood nothing of the game who, at this (de coup), would feel himself authorised merely to add on, that is, to add any old thing. He would add nothing, the seam wouldn't hold...The reading or writing supplement must be rigorously prescribed, but by the necessities of a game, by the logic of play, signs to which the system of all textual powers must be accorded and attuned (Derrida, 1981, p. 64).

Derrida's deconstructionism aims to draw out of a text an undismissable prescribed sign or signification. Such significations function within written texts and conform to language, or more specifically to its regulated function. The sign is not pursued in order to find the author's intention neither is it sought as meanings imposed by language and history. In essence, the signifier or the text, is the field of play in which language is uncovered as a chain of significations amidst a textual system that permits multiple interpretations and denies the dominance of any particular one.

By questioning the organizing principles of canonical texts, Derrida aims to place these principles in a new relation to each other, suggesting the possibility that complications can be debated rather than suppressed. Thus, deconstruction is used not to abolish truth, science, logic and philosophy, but to question how these concepts are present in texts and how they are employed to systematically exclude certain categories of thought and communication. The implications of a deconstructive reading are therefore not limited to the language of the text itself but can be extended to the political and social context in which the text is placed.

A deconstructive reading opens up the text to renewed debate concerning the limits of the text and the relationship between explicit and hidden textual levels. In investigating the limits of the text, the critic asks a number of questions, for example, why are certain authors or topics, excluded from the text? Why are certain themes never questioned, whereas other themes are condemned? Why, given a set of premises are certain conclusions not reached? The aim of such questions to assist the reader to understand the extent to which the text's objectivity and persuasiveness depend on a series of strategic exclusions.

On the question of power, deconstruction raises a problematic agenda. In critical theory, hegemonic relations are regarded as external dispositions, dispersed from traditional conceptions of monarchy and law. Subsequently, they are seen as counterproductive hegemonic relations. Power is exercised from above and explained in traditional terms of historical relations to monarchy and its conspiratorial vassals, the law and in the case of traditional European monarchies, the church. Foucault (1980) ties modern power to technology, still reducible to the representation of law, however it is power that is enforced not by right, but by technique and knowledge of modern technology. Here law is controlled by normalisation and not punishment and applies methods that at all levels go beyond the state and its apparatus.

Both Derrida and Foucault share the view that reflective acknowledgment of power relations does not amount to liberation from them and this view places in doubt the concepts of emancipation held in critical theory. Derrida perceives humanity as being bound within traditions through linguistically and unable go beyond stating what the difficulty is. Stating what the difficulty is, in Derrida's view, is stating the difficulty of stating, not overcoming the difficulty.

Analytic Strategies Used in Deconstruction

Though much has been referred to in recent years regarding deconstruction in postmodern research there is a noticeable scarcity of deconstruction strategies. Martin (1990, p. 355) provides a useful framework from which to begin the process of deconstruction.

• Dismantling a dichotomy, exposing it as a false distinction.

- Examining silences—what is not said.
- Attending to disruptions and contradictions, places where the text fails to make sense.
- Focusing on the element that is most alien to a text or a context as a means of deciphering implicit taboos—the limits to what is conceivable or permissible.
- Interpreting metaphors as a rich source of multiple meanings.
- Analysing 'double-entendres' that may point to an unconscious subtext, often sexual in content.
- Separating group-specific and more general sources of bias by 'reconstructing' the text with iterative substitution phrases.
- Exploring, with careful 'reconstructions' the unexpected ramifications and inherent limitations of minor policy changes.
- Using the limitations exposed by 'reconstruction' to explain the persistence of the status quo and the need for more ambitious change programs.

There are alternative practices that make available the evidence on which one's interpretations are based and attempt to move beyond the 'subject-become-object' status of the participant in relation to the researcher. These practices are identified by Opie (1992) as:

- The recognition of the limitations of the researcher's research and knowledge.
- The analytic reading of the participants' interview text, which demands reflexivity from the researcher.
- Some principles in relation to the incorporation of quotations from the participant's texts (what Opie calls 'writing in voices), including the criteria for the selection of quotations and whether the researcher should be solely responsible for interpretation.
- Issues of empowerment.

Deconstruction as Contested Terrain

Deconstruction as an approach to texts also has its limits. Derrida's difficult language serves as the first limiting factor: Many social scientists are impatient with an elusive parenthetical style that avoids the simplification of ideas. Derrida's refusal to offer a clear definition of the deconstructive process and its implications is consistent with his overall suspicion of abstraction and generalization. Those who dare to deconstruct a text must rely on their own understanding of the dare. Furthermore, to deconstruct a text they must rely on their own understanding of the gestures of deconstruction as practiced by Derrida.

Linstead (1993a) highlights the possibility that deconstruction may give rise to endless interpretive games and result in a kind of:

> ...easygoing pluralist tolerance, which leaves no room for significant disagreement on issues of principle or practice (Linstead 1993a, p. 109)

Derrida (1976) argues however, that deconstruction:

> ...is not easy and requires all the instruments of classical criticism. Without this recognition and this respect, critical production would risk developing in any direction at all and authorise itself to say almost anything. (p. 158)

What Derrida demonstrates is that language inevitably suppresses and privileges. It is not sufficient however, to acknowledge that this takes place, but examine what or who becomes privileged.

The tensions for the researcher in adopting deconstruction as a tool in research require brief reflection. In asking of every representation 'Is this fact?' without coming to any final conclusions (since there is not absolute legitimating 'truth'), there is a constant need to avoid relativistic paralysis. In using deconstruction, the researcher approaches social and organisational life through the text, entering into its terms and using them to disrupt any conventionalised consciousness of their significance. The researcher draws on a particular poststructuralist theory as a device to resuscitate the subordinate term of 'rigidity', to elevate it, and thus to amplify the silenced voices. This is a way of problematising the dominant understanding of 'flexibility' and rather than creating a new hierarchy, reconstructs a duality of awareness within conventional consciousness. Herein lies the tension. Because deconstruction requires subjectivity and reflexivity, it inevitably reveals what Martin (1990, p. 341) refers to as the 'I/eye/ideology' of the deconstructor as well as the deconstructed.

Such insights place in question the authority of the deconstructed account and the charge of the possibility of infinitude of interpretations and accounts. Linstead (1993a, p. 113) raises a number of questions in this regard in which the researcher needs time to consider and ultimately 'position' herself through her responses:

- With no claim to factual superiority, how can the researcher's account contest the accuracy of other accounts?
- How can it avoid the charge of nihilism if it recognises no absolute authority and all facts, values, and assumptions are undecidable?

- How can it enable choice between accounts if all are substitutable and none have priority?
- How can it deal with non-epistemological issues—ideology, politics, ethics, and morality—if its relativisation of the new leaves it no means to challenge the hegemony of the old?

Deconstruction and Sport Management Research

Our purpose in introducing deconstruction to sport management is to subvert the pretensions of positive theory as a theory of knowledge production. We believe that this school of sport management research exercises undue influence on the production of sport management knowledge. There is an apparent unwillingness to critically examine the political, ontological and epistemological assumptions that underlie research and the disciplining forces of a hegemonic academic elite within sport management. Our purpose therefore in supporting deconstruction is to hold positive theory intellectually accountable and to make clear the fact that knowledge production is always a political act.

Conclusion

Deconstruction involves tracing the limitations and self-contradictions that characterize complex texts. From a deconstructive perspective, writing is never neutral it always requires interpretation. Deconstruction may be particularly useful in undermining such standard textual claims as the objectivity of the argument. The aim of deconstruction is to open debate to complexities and issues that have been ignored or suppressed.

From a deconstruction perspective authors have not privileged access to the meaning of the texts they inscribe. Every deconstruction then is an ambiguous document that both celebrates and condemns its own test even as it points to other texts. Consequently, the arguments offered in this chapter have been designed to open debate on the ideological underpinnings of sport management theory.

Chapter 5

Discourse Analysis: A Framework for Thinking

> Different conversations, like different pictures of the same landscape, proceed alongside each other and each conversation is within other larger conversations.
>
> Brew (2001: 157)

What is Discourse?

The term discourse, within the context of this chapter, has a particular meaning. Prior (1988) notes that the concept of discourse is more often than not utilized within realist ontology. Discourse typically refers to a linguistic activity or to the construction of accounts in the form of speech or texts. Within this perspective, discourse is always about something. It is suggested therefore that out there is a universe of objects and here before us is a discourse on that universe. Discourse reports on the world and the task of sociology is often seen as unravelling of such reports or accounts (see for example, Mulkay 1985 and Prior, 1988, p. 91). Thus, discourse refers to intransitive objects (Bhaskar, 1979), which exist in a universe of independent of discourse.

Prior (1988) notes that in some recent strands of discourse analysis, including Foucault's (1972, 1978), the realist position is rejected from the outset. In contrast, 'the division between the word and the world is dissolved' (Prior, 1988, p. 92). Discourse is not merely about objects, but rather, constitutes them. In this respect, discourses 'construct the very objects to which they refer' (Prior, 1988, p. 92). The object and the discourse itself emerge together and are shaped by the social, cultural and institutional areas in which they make their appearance. It is within this context that the term discourse is used here.

It is important to note that a discourse does not constitute a single coherent lore of belief or practice, but rather, is formed by many people talking and acting at once, often in conflicting ways and who belong to different communities or fields; the political, the economic and so forth (Lemert & Gillan, 1982; Rajchman, 1985). Foucault (1972) refers to this dispersion of discourses and its intersections across fields as a discursive formation. He notes:

> Whenever one can describe, between a number of statements, such a system of dispersion, whenever, between objects, one can define a regularity (an order, correlations, positions and functioning's, transformations), we will say for the sake of convenience, that we are dealing with a discursive formation. (Foucault, 1972, p. 38)

In his analysis of discourse, Foucault is concerned with asking questions such as what rules permit certain statements to be made: what rules order these statement; and what rules enable us to identify statements as true or false? Thus, discourse in this context refers to a system of possibility of knowledge, or, ways of talking and thinking.

Foucault uses the principle of discourse to show how power relationships and subjectivity are constituted. Discourses are structuring mechanisms for social institutions, modes of thought and individual subjectivities. They are:

> ...practices that systematically form the objects of which they speak... Discourses are not about objects; they do not identify objects, they constitute them and in the process of doing so conceal their own invention (Foucault 1972, p. 49).

Foucault's notion of discourse therefore includes ideas, rituals and practice. Foucault suggests the first theoretical point was that discourse operates always within time. Discourse as a term concerns what at a given era is said, written, thought out of all the things that could be said, written and thought, the historically specific field of what is said. The second theoretical point was that discourse is not self-generating, for there are always historically specific practices, which form the controlling, selecting, organizing and redistributing procedures that structure, its production. Thus, within any era the play between practice and discourse ensures that the discursive field will be made up of a whole range of specific discourses, competing, overlapping, always subject to problems of definition, status and differentiation, emerging from old discourses and mutating into new (Foucault, 1972).

The significance of all this was the focus on discourse—represented a new order of thinking about language: the 'order of discourse'. For this intermediate 'order' had always been overlooked throughout the history of Western philosophy. Being mistaken as the transparent vehicle between thought and speech—between, in a longstanding philosophical opposition, the deep structure of language, meaning and truth (known in the ancient world as the Logos and to Saussure as 'langue') and the surface event of the word we speak or write ('Parole').

This apparently transparent vehicle Foucault (1972) argues, is in fact the bridge that traverses the otherwise unbridgeable chasm between deep structure and surface. It is what has constituted the possibility for communication, (i.e. of both deep structure and surface speaking), of both the social forms of language and the individual speaking subject.

The most substantial articulation of this pivotal argument comes in his 1970 inaugural address at the College de France; itself entitled 'The Order of Discourse' (Foucault, 1981). Here, Foucault aims to establish the theoretical centrality of discourse by showing that the whole logos-based approach to making sense and establishing truth since Plato makes no sense without it.

That approach as Foucault (1981) argues has been historically focused on establishing 'the division between true and false' by means of establishing the correctness of the surface word 'the utterance itself, its meaning, its form, its object, its relation to its reference' (p. 54). By that focus the role of discourse has been suppressed, as perceived surface correctness has been taken as the guarantee that underlying truth has been captured (and so by extension that the thinker who argues correctly is the philosopher-king or 'sovereign rational subject). Over history certainly, the forms of our will to truth have differed, (i.e. 'in the history of the range of objects known, of the functions and positions of the knowing subject, of the material, technical and instrumental investments of knowledge p. 55). But they all moved in the Platonic frame of reference, pursuing the same will to truth as surface correctness. Thus, discourse has from the time of Plato been squeezed out. In this way, philosophies have all failed to understand discourse's constitutive role in enabling them to speak in the first place.

Foucauldian Discourse Analysis

Foucauldian discourse analysis views discourse as relations of power/knowledge encoded in the social processes of language and action. Foucauldian style discourse analysis has also been referred to as genealogy, power analytics, critical hermeneutics or critical ethnography, although there are those who maintain that there are differences among these approaches. It is important to note that a power analytic focuses more on the power relations in a discourse, a genealogy focuses more on the historical component of a discourse, a critical hermeneutic analysis focuses on the social meanings of a discourse that perpetuate oppression and a critical ethnography focuses on the identification of oppression as expressed by a particular situated group of people. Foucauldian discourse analysis includes all of these elements.

He argues that discourse, knowledge and power are so closely interrelated that a field of discourse is co-extensive with a field of power. In fact, Foucault often used the phrase 'power/knowledge' with respect to discourse. Thus using a Foucauldian perspective, it is possible to explore the links between knowledge, power and resultant discourses. An analysis of these links reveals that claims to knowledge by exponents of certain dominant discourses are in fact, claims to power (Foucault, 1980).

All discourses, in the Foucauldian view, contain internal contradictions. Analysis of the contradictions and silences in a discourse are important elements in a Foucauldian discourse analysis. Because of the historically situated nature of all discourses, the internal contradictions 'make sense' only with respect to a specific context. This makes it problematic to claim that a discourse analysis describes 'what is really going on' within a discourse because the analyst co-exists with the discourse she or he is analysing. Consequently, the purpose of discourse analysis is to describe the contradictions and puzzles as they become apparent, as a 'tool for radical political action' (Foucault, 1980, p. 205). This is say, that a discourse analysis recognizes itself to be a historically situated interpretation of a historically situated discourse related to a discourse and power for the people involved. It is important therefore, to describe the discourse in the contest of the lives of historically situated participants, because discourse both describes and is productive of lived experience in the hermeneutic sense.

A Foucauldian style discourse analysis is sometimes referred to as an analytic because it seeks the conditions that make possible the analyses practiced in the discipline (Kusch, 1991). Discourse analysis decomposes statements and their context-dependent interpretation into context-dependent categories called subjects, concepts and strategies. Discourse analysis does not decompose statements into elements and abstract universal rules of formation, as do structural methods of analysis.

Therefore, the discourse analyst does not posit a universal meaning to a discourse or to its context-dependent analysis. Rather, discourse analysis seeks the regularities that determine the operation of a specific historically situated discourse, including social practices as well as the rules of written and spoken discourse. Such practices include institutions, events, practices, politics, economics, demographics, media, gestures, clothing, style, habits, terminology and the range of roles to be fulfilled by human subjects (Foss and Gill, 1987).

Foucault (1983) stresses that a discourse analysis concerns itself with the following power/knowledge issues: (1) the 'system of differentiations or privileged access to the discourse; (2) the types of objectives of one group of adherents over another; (3) the means of bringing power relations into being that reveals surveillance systems, threats and dismissals; (4) 'forms of institutionalization' such as bureaucratic structures; and (5) degree of rationalization required to support power arrangements.

This is to say, when analysing a discourse it is crucial to consider what conflicting groups of people are saying within the discourse. Who gets listened to most often and why, what the hidden agendas are, who gets chastised for their deeds or writings, how the discourse becomes widespread and to whom, and how the existence of the discourse is said to be necessary and to whom.

Foucauldian discourse analysis is not a historical method for the production of causal arguments. It may be characterized instead as the interpretation of historically situated discourse arising from practical concerns regarding power and resistance.

The process of a Foucauldian style discourse analysis involves careful reading of entire bodies of text and other organizing systems (such as taxonomies, commentaries and conference transcriptions) in relation to one another, in order to interpret patterns, rules, assumptions, contradictions, silences, consequences, implications and inconsistencies (Weedon, 1987). The product identifies and names language processes and social practices that people use to construct their understanding of social life, that necessarily serves either to reproduce or challenge the distribution of power as it currently exists (Weedon, 1987).

The product of a discourse analysis shows how discourses are constructed, circulated and played out. Discourse analysis includes a focus on oppression and also identifies potential discourses of resistance through which people may construct subject position that challenge the dominant discourses. Discourses analysis may involve identification of several related discourses available to people in a given social context at a given time.

Discourse Analysis and Sport Management

The potential contribution of a Foucauldian style discourse analysis to the discipline of sport management is twofold. First, discourse analysis would provide an approach suitable for addressing such notions as; (1) the taken-for-grantedness of specific sport management practices; (2) the history of sport management practices; (3) the vested interest of authorized voices; (4) the rules of evidence used to formulate and structure discussions; (5) the rules by evidence used to produce explanations and the rules of which topics are dismissed from inquiry. Examples of questions that could guide this form of discourse analysis include. Who are considered authorities in sport management and why? What discourses is contained in sport management texts and journals? How do we justify sport management as a discipline? When you submit an article on sport management to be published, what changes are commonly made and by whom?

A second area in which discourse analysis can contribute to the discipline is by providing a way to analyse power in sport management. Examples of issues that would benefit greatly from the power perspective provided by discourse analysis, include the discourses of theory, professionalism, practice, gender, communication and oppression to name only a few. An examination of these issues would contribute to the further development of sport management as an academic discipline. However, to achieve this we must first address how sport management theory and discourse analysis can be used to provide a greater understanding of the profession.

Sport Management Theory as Discourse

With respect to sport management, Foucauldian analysis can illuminate the mechanisms and techniques used by sport management to legitimise its own knowledge claims and the various, often competing, discourses embedded in sport management knowledge. They can reveal the nature of the interplay between sport management 'experts' and practitioners. For example, in sport management the technocratic discourse operates in such a way as to limit the sport mangers' perception of the nature of management practice. The power afforded to the technocratic/managerial discursive framework is such that it is very difficult for sport management practitioners to move away from a management approach to a reflective practitioner. As such the discursive formation of the managerial model both legitimises this approach to sport management practice and limits other forms of possibility.

The product of a discourse analysis includes a description of the internal rules and ideological elements of a particular discourse, plus documentation of the 'conditions of its existence'. Questions that would illuminate the conditions of existence for the discourse of sport management theory, for example, would include the following. What kinds of practices or discourses had to be in place before the discourse of sport management theory could be constructed? What social practices and power arrangements are necessary for the discourse of sport management theory to continue? What implicit rules are there in the discourse of sport management theory that helps to validate its existence?

In such analysis there is a dynamic relationship between power and 'truth' where truth is a product of dominant discursive frameworks shaped and defined by power, whilst power is legitimated on the basis of expert ownership of such 'truth'. For example, the scientific/management model is regularly described as neutral and value free. So hegemonic is this notion of objectivity, that the underlying relations of power embedded in 'true' concepts such as objectivity and neutrality are not exposed. Foucault extends the conceptualisation of power from the realm of the ideological, to figuring in the very production of the instruments for the formation and accumulation of knowledge. In such an analysis, knowledge is not identical to ideology but in fact precedes ideology. Further, dominant discourses figure in both the development and the continuation of social truths.

From Foucault's perspective all discourses are merely perspectives. If one discourse has more value than another this is not because of its intrinsic properties as truth but because of the role that discourse plays in constituting practices. Discourses produce not 'truth' but 'truth effects' (i.e. they organize and constitute the world in particular ways). These effects are not contingent on whether the discourse is oppressive or liberating. Any discursive regime (and human existence is unthinkable without one) implies a particular exercise of power. Power not only represses but it also makes possible the knowledge that constitutes culture—any culture. Foucault argues for the power effect of knowledge rather than its truth-value. The notion of ideology critique is misleading in that it promises a truth not distorted through the effects of domination. For Foucault such a notion would be an impossibility.

Discourse analysis draws attention to the discursive construction of sport management knowledge and practices, the point is not to replace one set of categories with another, but to focus on differences and marginality, thus expanding different theoretical understandings and facets of experience. Poststructural sport management discourses inquiry does not propose a new 'paradigm' in the sense of value-free truth seeking, the concern is with 'intertextualism', which involves the generation of new positions to resist or question existing discourse.

Sport Policy as Discourse

Prunty (1985) notes a precise definition of policy is elusive, as the term has no standard use and is riddled with ambiguity. Prunty (1985) initially describes a broad category of distinction, denoting policy as either substantive or procedural. Substantive policy relates to policy that denotes directives for action, whilst the category of procedural policy denotes responsibilities for action or the processes guiding action.

Grimley (1986) notes that 'policy is… an expression of values by a politically dominant group' (p. 20). When considered from this perspective, policy loses some of its innocence as a neutral conveyor of procedures and undertakings to be implemented for the common good and can be viewed as a vehicle which promotes the values, understandings and ultimately the interests of a particular group. When sport policy impacts on the practice of sport management it is essentially a political exercise, in that from a number of possibilities certain views will be chosen and enshrined in policy documents.

The reading of policy documents as texts that represent certain views of reality can inform our analysis. The way in which policies are developed, represent reality, are spoken about and though about, is the product of dominant discursive frameworks or discourses by which we mean certain ways of thinking or talking about reality (Foucault, 1977). These dominant discourses are themselves the product of social, historical and other structural influences. The development and maintenance of such dominant discursive frameworks shapes the way in which sport managers and others think about sport management and the practice of sport management.

Thus what is not said or embodied in policy that shapes sport management is of as much interest as what is present or said. As Foucault (1980) points out when analysing how the social body, the sport manager in this instance, comes to be constituted and understood, there is in play at any one time

> …a thorough heterogeneous ensemble consisting of discourses, institutions, architectural forms, regulatory decisions, laws, administrative measures, scientific statements, philosophical, moral and philanthropic propositions—in short the said as much as the unsaid. (p. 194)

When considered from a Foucauldian perspective such as proposed here, policy could be viewed as a vehicle that promotes the ideology of a certain group. Foucauldian perspectives problematise the relationship between power and knowledge and how that relationship is evident in the social world.

Policy analysis as a field of study has suffered from an uncertain identity and vagueness of conceptualisation. A Foucauldian policy analysis aims to expose sources of domination, repression and exploitation that are entrenched in, and legitimated by policy. Thus a policy analysis goes beyond analysing the content and implementation of policies to examine how those policies reflect certain understandings of reality in the first instance. Policy analysis is therefore overtly political in that it attempts to expose favoured values and social arrangements and the sources of power and control underpinning them and hegemonic technologies that restrain human consciousness and emancipation.

One focus of such an analysis is upon the policy as text, incorporating an analysis of the values, interests and assumptions characterised through the scope, intentions, and language of the policy document. The questions raised related to 'whose needs, values and preferences are represented' and 'on what basis are (they) validated as being appropriate and good'? Thus, analysis of the language used in the text of the policy unveils the underlying values, assumptions and ideologies that underpin the policy. However, a focus solely upon the language and text of policy can become technical and functionalist if it fails to consider the processes associated with policy development and implementation. Further, text is always produced in social settings where a great deal more than language is present.

A discourse approach must of necessity take account of the processes of text (policy) production as well as the actual test (policy) itself. This involves investigation and examination of the processes by which the need for policy is determined and communicated, and the processes by which policy is developed (i.e. policy committees and how these committees are constituted and conducted) implemented and reviewed.

Therefore in viewing sport management focused policy documents as constituted by certain discourses a Foucauldian policy analysis requires analysis of the relationship between texts, processes in the development of those texts and the social conditions in which the texts are produced and operate. This analysis of social conditions must consider both the immediate conditions of the situational context, and the seemingly more remote yet ever present conditions of the institutional and social structures within which the policy is constituted. Thus in relation to sport policy, it is necessary to not only examine the text of the policy, but also the structural aspects of policy development (i.e. the relationship between processes of production and implementation).

From a Foucauldian perspective text (policy) is viewed as an outcome of historical and political conditions. Thus, a Foucauldian approach to policy analysis requires examination of the social milieu surrounding text (policy) production in order to illuminate the nature of the relationships between processes of text (policy) production, and how they are constituted through and constitutive of dominant ideologies.

It should be clear that it would be incomplete to describe the evolution of sport policy in a particular context without considering the social structure of the culture from which the sport policy arises. Some questions that could be asked in such an inquiry include. What cultural practices gave rise to the sport policy? What power relations were at work in the politics of sport policy development? Were there gender issues involved? What political issues have influenced sport policy?

Critique of Discourse Analysis

Critics accustomed to the positivist paradigm within which much research takes place may assert that discourse analyses are too subjective, relying almost entirely upon the particular researchers reading of a text. Discourse analysis theory openly acknowledges the inevitability of a theoretical position being context and observer specific. Indeed, the role of discourse analysis as a critical tool requires that the researchers particular perspective be made explicit.

There are a few ways of validating one's assertions in discourse analysis. The extensive use of the actual textual material used in the analysis is important for it allows others to assess the researchers' interpretations and follow the reasoning process from data to conclusions. In discourse analysis the text is not a dependent variable, or an illustration of another point, but an example of the data itself. Another powerful criterion of validity is whether an analytic scheme can make sense of new kinds of discourse and generate new understandings. Evidence of other interpretations and cognitive processing are also important as they provide a deeper insight into how text can assist in creating different perceptions of the world for others.

It should be clearly understood that the analysis of discourse analysis does not involve simply the cataloguing and observation of patterns, but also includes a critical dimension. The very characteristic that defines discourse as a poststructural activity is its goal in identifying cultural hegemony and the manner by which it is reproduced.

Concluding Comments

The discipline of sport management has taken its place in universities world wide without a long history of allegiance to an established philosophical perspective or social theory. Sport management is presently in an enviable position of having a widely informed choice among philosophical approaches as models for teaching, practice and research.

The application of discourse analysis as a methodology for sport management inquiry provides our discipline with the opportunity to construct alternative perspectives on power/knowledge. Such an addition to sport management inquiry would therefore appear well justified.

Chapter 6

Action Research: A Cautionary Note for Sport Management

What is Action Research?

Action research has been defined as a form of research carried out by practitioners in order to improve the rationality and justice of (1) their own social and educational practices, (2) their understanding of these practices and, (3) the situations in which the practices are carried out (Kemmis, 1995). It involves a spiral of cycles of:

- planning a change;
- acting and observing the process and consequences of the change;
- reflecting of these processes and consequences;
- replanning;
- acting and observing; and
- reflecting

Kemmis (1995) further identifies five features of action research:

1   Action research is a social process it deliberately explores the relationship between the realms of the individual and the social. It recognises that 'no individuation is possible without socialization, and no socialization is possible without individuation' (Habermas, 1972, p. 26).

2   Action research is participatory: it engages people in examining their knowledge (understandings, skills and values) and interpretive categories (the ways they interpret themselves and their action in the social and material world).

3   Action research is practical and collaborative: it engages people in examining the acts that link them with others in social interaction.

4   Action research is emancipatory. It aims to help people recover an awareness of and release themselves from the constraints of irrational, unproductive, unjust, and unsatisfying social structures which limit their self-development and self-determination.

5. Action research is critical. It aims to help people recover an awareness of and release themselves from the constraints embedded in the social media through which they interact. Their language (discourses), their modes of work, and the social relationships of power (in which they experience affiliation and difference, inclusion and exclusion—relationships in which, grammatically speaking, they interact with others in the first or second or third person).

Although this provides some insight into action research to fully understand it and its implications for sport management research it is necessary to explore its origins.

Origins and Development of Action Research

The intellectual origins of action research can be traced back through Schwab's (1999) concept of practical reasoning, Kolb's (1984) experiential learning cycle, Schon's (1983) reflective practitioner, and to Lewin who coined the term 'action research' (Kemmis, 1995). However, the history of action research over the last 50 years is complex containing many strands, emphases, nuances and variations between national and operational contexts.

MacTaggart (1991) defines four generations of action research. The 1st generation is seen as originating with Lewin, and developing through the late 1950s in the educational sphere in America. The 2nd generation developed within Britain from the 1960s through to the 1980s. The 3rd generation originated in the 1980s with a call for a more critical basis within Australia and Europe. The 4th generation developed in Australia with emancipatory action research as the culmination of the previous three generations.

The fourth generation of action research owes much of its origins to the previous generations. Jennings (1995) suggests the third generation with its call for a 'more explicitly 'critical' and 'emancipatory' action research approaches to research' was the real impetus for the fourth generation. It was here that the influences of the work of the German Philosopher and Sociologist Jurgen Habermas began to filter into action research.

Habermas (1971) saw three kinds of cognitive interests inherent in the way 'in which knowledge is constituted', which for Habermas meant that 'knowing could not be a dis-interested act'. These cognitive interests: (a) Technical—which corresponds to the adaptation of knowledge to 'technical dispositions, i.e. the empirical-analytical sciences; (b) Practical—which corresponds to the adaptations of knowledge 'to the arrangements of practical life'; (c) Emancipatory—which corresponds to the adaptation of knowledge to 'emancipation from naturalist constraint', (Habermas, 1971). The influence of Habermas' can be seen in the terminology that the fourth generation has adopted. The fourth generation distinguishes three types of action research: (1) emancipatory, (2) practical, and (3) technical, (MacTaggart, 1991).

1. Emancipatory Action Research

Emancipatory action research according to MacTaggart (1991, p. 30) could be defined in two ways. First, as '[involving] a group of practitioners accepting responsibility for its 'own emancipation' from the dictates of irrationality, injustice, alienation and unfulfillment'. Second, as 'the activity of a self-leading group aimed at developing new practices and/or changing the constraints with a shared radical consciousness'.

According to MacTaggart (1991) emancipatory action research extends beyond the interpretation of meanings for participants to an understanding of the social, political, and economic conditions, which allow meanings to be as they are. In terms of knowledge and human interests, emancipatory action research is clearly aimed at criticism and liberation through a process of critical reflection. The human interest served by such practices is that of 'collective emancipation' (p. 30).

The main points of emancipatory action research according to Carr and Kemmis (1986) that are of equal importance are:
- bridging the gap between theory and practice;
- the epistemological understanding that the practitioners possess valid knowledge;
- participation and equality of those involved within the situation;
- practitioners critically reflecting on their own practices;
- the empowerment of the practitioners;
- democratically chosen actions are implemented;
- communication, which implies a dialogues between participants; and
- a cyclic process of 'planning, action, observation and reflection.

What these points imply is a rejection of the positivistic and scientific conceptions of epistemology, objectivity, research and social reality. This also implies a rejection of the positivistic conception of the formulation or development of covering laws or generalisations to explain social reality. The methodology is chosen and implemented by the practitioners themselves, which implies it is situation specific. Thus emancipatory action research is more than simple radical critique—it demands action.

2. Practical Action Research

Practical action research has many of the points of emancipatory action research discussed above. In a practical action research project the aim is the ultimate autonomy of the profession practitioners themselves to conceive and implement projects on their own. To be critically informed self-reflecting practitioners.

3. Technical Action Research

Technical action research could be defined as '[aiming] to contribute both to the practical concerns of people in an immediate problematic situation and to the goals of social science by joint collaboration with a mutually acceptable ethical framework', (Rapopart, 1970, p. 499).

It usually consists of a researcher who within the context of a topic of interest will either construct and define a problem or have a problem defined by a client. The researcher will then formulate the methodology to be used and conduct the research. The data gathered would then be interpreted and analysed by the researcher, who will then write up the research, which will add to existing knowledge by outlining the new practices to be implemented (Kemmis, 1995). An example of this form of action research is the work of the [Tavistock Institute of Human Relations] or the 1950s and 1960s.

Another form of action research—Participatory Action Research (PAR)—should also be highlighted. It had its beginnings in the 1950s in America, where a PAR network fought to keep it alive. However, its influence dwindled and it was not really taken seriously until the 1980's (Whyte, 1991). In PAR practitioners are co-researchers throughout, there is not external imposition of change. It is for this reason that PAR is credited with democratizing (Van Manen, 1990) or proletarianizing science, that is, eschewing the traditional elitist view of research and researchers by providing practitioners with opportunities and tools to research and thereby improve their own practices. In addition, the very nature of PAR enables and encourages their development and continuous learning throughout the change process (Tripp, 1993).

To begin with, because they are involved in the research cycle from the outset practitioners' decision making skills should be enhanced. Their involvement in diagnosis strategy development and implementation and ongoing evaluation should furnish them with decision-making opportunities. In addition, because problem diagnosis and strategy development is collaboratively agreed the interpersonal skills of practitioners should also be enhanced.

PAR seems to encompass facets of technical, practical and emancipatory action research. That is, first, it is usually defined as being participatory yet the degree of participation and equality are not set. Second, there is usually a degree of facilitation, and third, the problem may be defined by the researcher (MacTaggart, 1989). From a fourth generation perspective the honorific 'participatory' is superfluous because fourth generation action research is by definition participatory.

Adaptation of Action Research for the Social Sphere

This section of the chapter will give brief descriptions of some adaptations of action research. These are: (1) The Tavistock Institute of Human Relations (Rapoport, 1970); (2) Action Science (Argyris, Putman and McLain-Smith, 1990); then it will give a more thorough account of (3) Convergent Interviewing, (Dick, 1993b).

1. Tavistock Institute of Human Relations

Rapoport (1970) defines action research, which is seen as an alternative to other methodologies as:

> [aiming] to contribute both to the practical concerns of people in an immediate problematic situation and to the goals of social science by joint collaboration with a mutually acceptable ethical framework (p. 499).

The 'Tavistock experience' (as Rapoport calls it) of action research entails the client (usually a corporation or firm) hiring the services of a researcher to conduct research into a defined problem within a sector or department of the corporation. The problem (or problematic situation) is usually defined by the client and the role of the researcher is that of an objective change agent who would conduct the research, formulate changes to practices for the company to implement. The role of the researcher would then be that of an academic who contributes knowledge to the social sciences.

2. Action Science

Argyris et al. (1990) describes Action Science as 'an inquiry into how human beings design and implement action in relation to one another' (p. 1). They expand on this further when they suggest action research is also 'a conception of practical knowledge that goes beyond the common conception of choosing means to achieve predetermined ends' (p. 1). For Argyris et al (1990) 'action science' is a science of action that 'takes its meanings' from being contrasted to pure science, thus it is perceived as an alternative methodology. Action Science strives to both inform action in concrete situations and to test general theory. Action Science also recognizes the gap between theory and practice hence it has the aim of producing knowledge that can inform practice and to all to existing knowledge.

3. Convergent Interviewing

For Dick (1993a) convergent interviewing is a technique of action research, which is viewed as an alternative methodology to the traditional methodologies for collecting and analysing data. Dick describes action research as '[research] done in field settings with a view to bring about change and at the same time adding to the appropriate body of knowledge' (p. 5). He describes convergent interviewing as:

> [consisting] of long interviews in which the content is unstructured…[though] the interview itself uses a process which is somewhat structured…[and] as the interviews proceed the questions become more specific…[with] later interviews becom[ing] more focused…[with] the interviewers develop[ing] an interpretation of the data, which is very tentative early in the procedure (p. 1).

For Dick (1993b) there are two versions of action research: (1) action is the primary focus and research is a by-product; (2) research is the primary focus. Within both versions the researcher or consultant is employed by a client (a person or organisation) to conduct research to change a problematic situation. The client or the researcher usually defines the problem situation, the methodology, and goals and the researcher conducts the interpretation of the data. Within both versions the role of the researcher is that of a 'change agent'.

Cyclic phenomenon continues and more interviews are conducted until a clear picture has emerged. Within this cyclic process two kinds of patterns are sought: (1) 'patterns of convergence or agreement'; (2) patterns of 'discrepancy and disagreement. It is these patterns that help define the questions and the directions for each interview, and provide the researcher with 'objective methods' for 'refining subjective data'.

Commissioned Intervention

In this type of action research change agents ('experts') are engaged to facilitate the implementation of new management policies or to facilitate the application of research findings to practice. This approach to action research assists in the implementation of externally determined change and in turn, places practitioners in the position as the subjects of change. On the other hand, practitioner ownership of the proposed intervention may be absent. In this case subject practitioners may sabotage the change process. It should be noted however, that because commissioned intervention places participants in the position of subjects, critical action researchers might deny that it is action research at all.

Limitations and Practical and Theoretical Problems
of Action Research

This following critically analyses the theory and practice of the transposition into social inquiry of: (1) Emancipatory Action Research; (2) Practical Action Research; and (3) Technical Action Research.

1. Emancipatory Action Research

Emancipatory action research as described previously has been influenced by critical social theory and therefore has made redundant the role of the social scientist. This outcome alone makes the transposition of emancipatory action research into social inquiry problematic. The influence of Habermas, who believed the project of modernity was the 'unfinished project' of the enlightenment, has meant that emancipatory action research is very much enmeshed in the project of 'the enlightenment' (Habermas, 1987). The ideals of 'the enlightenment', such as progress, reason, rationality, freedom, and equality are the ideals of action research (Berstein, 1976). However, the enlightenment was asymmetrical in that it privileged only one side of the dichotomy, for example—rationality over irrationality

(Baumon, 1991). Yet one side of the dichotomy is defined by its opposite, i.e. equality by inequality, rationality by irrationality, hence for one to exist the other must also exist. Further, from the postmodernist perspective because these ideals are hard to live up to there is a production of a 'conflict of identity' when the identity oscillates between the ideal and its opposite (Bauman, 1995).

Kemmis (1991) in *Action Research in Postmodernisms* takes a quasi-postmodernist stance by suggesting that the recent debate about action research has been structured to sharply around dichotomies. Kemmis argues that we should not think in dichotomies, that is, in black or white, but should admit the greyness in between. Kemmis (1991) also states that action research is not utopian, yet the very ideals on which it is founded are based on the assumption of progress to an idea. He also expresses his 'impatience' with advocates and critics 'of action research which are more concerned with the methodology and theory of action research than they are with the problems of social and educational life' (p. 61).

Kemmis (1985), in *Action Research and the Politics of Reflection*, argues that the 'enlightenment…[has] failed thus far to achieve a rational, just, and fulfilling world order' (p. 139). This statement seems quite out of place considering action research is founded on the principles of the enlightenment. Another interesting contradiction within action research is that it is perceived as an alternative to the methodologies that maintain the status quo, and is also based upon the same ideals as those ideals that maintain the status quo. Furthermore, emancipatory action research relies on the practitioner possessing a familiarity with the concept of research and an access to information (Carr & Kemmis, 1986). However, with the transposition of emancipatory action research into the sphere of social enquiry social actors may not have this familiarity with the concept of research and may not have access to information. Hence, it could be quite problematic in practice in that if the social actors are guided towards this familiarity and information, to what degree of bias are the social actors guided.

Emancipatory action research in sport management relies on the equality of participants and democratically chosen outcomes. Meeting these ideals on the small scale may be possible, however, this may be more problematic on a larger scale within the sphere of social enquiry. Carr and Kemmis (1986) have contributed to the view that limits action research to a 'narrow model of method' by not emphasising the applicability of action research to 'large scale level'. This highlights the difficulties to large-scale projects within the sphere of social enquiry. This implies that there has to be a motivation to change—a willingness to participate; democratically chosen change; participation and equality of all those involved within the community or communities where the change will be implemented. With the increase in scale of study there will equally be an increase in the difficulties that these points highlight.

Emancipatory action research also questions the existing practices because they do not operate within a vacuum, may be distorted by ideologies, institutional bureaucracy, etc. Part of the critical self-reflection process is to discern the influences, which have distorted the practices, and to seek alternatives or to improve existing practices (MacTaggart, 1991). However, the new practices will not operate within a vacuum and hence they also may eventually be distorted. Therefore, the action research process must be a continuous process and not just a one off research project. Further, the process of critical self-reflection implies that the practitioner can move outside the ideologies and institutions and not have their reflection distorted by ideologies etc. However, the practitioner will, like the practices, not operate within a vacuum, hence it is unlikely that all the self-reflection will be free from ideological influences (MacTaggart, 1991). Hence, the ideals on which action research is defined are not universals that are set for all time; they are fluid and interpreted by ideologies. It is the people who use action research who interpret the ideals. Therefore, action research is not a theory and methodology that can be picked up and used by anyone like other cognitive theories and methodologies. It is a theory and method that is interpreted by those who use it.

Within the sphere of sport management emancipatory action research can serve the practitioners as an alternative to traditional methods of research and aid sport managers with improving their practices. However, because action research does not critically reflect upon its own the ideals, that is of the enlightenment, and the fact that it has made redundant the role of the social scientist, emancipatory action research is not a replacement to other methodologies within the sphere of social enquiry.

2. Practical Action Research

Practical action research derives its honorific title by the fourth generation of action research. The cognitive interest of knowledge within practical action research being linked to the 'practical', in Habermasian terms (Habermas, 1971).

Practical action research uses a facilitator, an outsider, as a 'process consultant' who 'establishes relationships with the practitioners and helps them to articulate their values and concerns to plan and monitor action and to evaluate the action and its effects (MacTaggart, 1991). The role of the facilitator is problematic in that it could still be that of a specialist, with specialist knowledge, who directs the course of the research. Within this respect practical action research runs the risk of being co-opted by the positivist epistemological assumptions action research challenges (Carr, 1995). The role of the facilitator is also problematic in the sense that to what degree is the facilitator able to guide the participants? Further, to what degree will this influence or bias be acknowledged?

This raises the questions: Who initiated the research? What role does the facilitator play? What are the goals and motives behind the research? What is the role of the facilitator? When the answers to these questions are returned with the researcher as the main character then the status of the research as action research must be questioned (MacTaggart, 1991).

Practical action research is also open to the same social engineering criticisms as technical and emancipatory action research, such as ethical questions about the role of the researcher and the nature of the change.

MacTaggart (1991) argues that within practical action research the professional researcher owns the theory, or crucial aspects of it. Practical action research, as with emancipatory, relies on a familiarity with research by the social actors and on unrestricted access to information sources. This familiarity and access within the sphere of social enquiry may not be present. This also raises the question of how the facilitator aids the practitioners in accessing theoretical material on both action research and on aspects of social theory. This is problematic within the sphere of social enquiry in that the informative material required for critical-self-reflection on social and institutional influences may be restricted to a certain framework.

When emancipatory, technical and practical action research are analysed with reference to the enlightenment and positivism it is evident they have some difficulties as an alternative methodology for social inquiry in sport management. That is not to say that the traditional research methods do not have inherent problems within their framework. It is to say that action research as an alternative methodology for sport management enquiry does not provide a suitable and justifiable alternative yet.

3. Technical Action Research

The reason why technical action research has been given the honorific of 'technical by the fourth generation of action research is due to the work of Habermas. The cognitive knowledge interest which Habermas terms the 'technical' refers to way in which the interest of the researcher is positioned within a certain—empirical-analytic-view to knowledge, research and the world. The fourth generation has discerned that the interests within technical action research are more akin to the technical than the emancipatory or practical interests.

Technical action research, as described earlier, is more prone to the criticism of the ideals of the enlightenment than is emancipatory action research. That is, within technical action research it is the researcher who decides how the ideals are to be interpreted. The implications of this for social inquiry, with regards to social engineering, cannot be ignored. That is, there could be a political agenda behind the research which could lead to undemocratic outcomes whiles reinforcing existing inequalities or developing new inequalities.

Technical action research, like that exemplified by 'the Tavistock experience' and 'convergent interviewing' is not by the fourth generation perspective action research (Dick, 1993b-). That is the problem; the methodology, the interpretation and the action outcome are set by the researcher. Again, according to Dick the principles of the enlightenment (progress etc.) upon which action research is based are not questioned. In fact, some are ignored such as equality and democracy. The implications of this cannot be ignored for the sake of an alternative methodology.

Dick (1997) argues that participation in action research is not 'all-or-none' and that 'there is a continuum which ranges from the barest contact to a situation where the client does the research. In the following papers Dick (1992, 1993a, 1993b, 1995, 1997) has interpreted the meaning of action research from the title of action research, thus he interprets action research as either research with the primary goal of action or research with the primary goal of research. However, this approach widens the gap between action research theory and practice by taking or re-interpreting only what is wanted and leaving the rest. Dick (1993a) has reduced action research to simplistic icons that are used to characterise it. Thus, he has taken some the principles of action research, (i.e. critical reflection, the cyclic process), and incorporated them into a positivistic framework. The challenge to the positivist epistemological claim that the specialists and not the practitioners possess valid knowledge is left behind. The knowledge possessed by the practitioners is treated as mere data to be interpreted. Furthermore, within convergent interviewing the critical reflection and the cyclic process is limited to the researcher. What convergent interviewing actually does is to silence the practitioner's voice. That is, it is only the researcher who critically reflects and interprets, which puts the researcher in the role of a specialist. This in turn treats the 'respondents' within the interviews as a mere source of data that can be analysed and interpreted by the specialist. This means convergent interviewing is a monologue, it does not allow for a dialogue between practitioner and practitioner, nor between practitioners and researcher. Hence, true communication is left out of convergent interviewing, and indeed out of technical action research (Dick 1993a). This has the effect of widening the gap between theory and practice rather than bridging it, and also re-instates the methodological and theoretical ideology that sets the agenda for theory and practice. This is the very ideology that practitioners are challenging when advocating and formulating action research (Carr & Kemmis, 1986). This can be seen within convergent interviewing and the Tavistock experience. The outside researcher can be contracted by the client, conduct their research, formulate actions to be implemented and then go on to the next research project. The problem inherent in this is that the researcher does not have to live with the implemented actions nor do they have to live with their consequences. Whereas in emancipatory action research it is the practitioners who choose the action to be implemented and it is they who must live with the consequences of those actions. Within technical action research the goals of the research project are formulated outside the practices of the practitioner (Dick, 1993a). This means that the goals and motives may be that of the client ('extrinsic' motives), or that of the researcher ('intrinsic' motives), or both (Sarantokos, 1993). Within the Tavistock experience the goals and motives are that of the client and researcher. This in itself according to Sarantokos may be problematic in that the client or even the researcher may have reasons to hide their real goals and motives and mislead certain interest groups. In the case of the client, the goals and motives are usually to improve a problematic situation that the client has defined. In the case of the researcher the goals and motives are the improvement of the problematic situation and to contribute to the existing knowledge within the social sciences with a view to discovering generalisations or covering laws. The latter is a purely theoretical goal. This is a particularly positivistic stance on the part of the researcher one that does not fit into action research that has goals that are pragmatic.

Technical action research, or for that matter emancipatory and practical is situation specific. It is concerned with the practices of the participant practitioners (i.e. sport managers, and not with the practices of another group, i.e. members of a sports club). Each situation will have specific nuances, practices, ideological distortions, practitioners and behaviours that will apply to only those within the action research project at hand. There will of course be similarities between practitioners with the same idea of professional practices, however, any attempt to make generalisations tends to silence the voices of the practitioners, which is what action research argues (Carr & Kemmis, 1986).

Dick (1993b) incorporates convergence and discrepancy as objective methods of interpreting subjective data. Convergence utilises a form of the positivistic conception of the principle of verification, which tries to see patterns of convergence or agreement or truth. Discrepancy utilises a form of Karl Poppers falsification principle (Popper, 1990), which seeks discrepancy or disagreement. Both convergence and discrepancy provide criteria for deciding whether to analyse the particular data further or to discard them. This incorporation of the positivists conception of truth, objectivity, epistemology, and in the cases of action science, convergent interviewing, and the Tavistock experience, a science which will provide covering laws, merely widens the gap between the theory and practice of action research itself through their re-interpretations of action research. For these reasons, technical action research (especially convergent interviewing, action science, and the Tavistock experience) does not provide a suitable and justifiable alternative to other methodologies in the sphere of social enquiry. These also raise the ethical questions of social engineering when the researcher and/or client control the research.

Concluding Comments

Within this chapter action research has been positioned within the spheres of social inquiry. Following this chapter has; first, from a fourth generation point of view described briefly the development of emancipatory action research, and described the varieties of action research and adaptations of action research. Second, the chapter has critically analysed the limitations, theoretical and practical problems of the transposition action research into the sphere of social enquiry. Within this analysis, it has been shown that due to the way that action research has been re-interpreted, sometimes within the pre-existing paradigms, (i.e. positivism), it has broadened the gap between the theory and practice of action research. Additionally, because the ideals of the enlightenment, upon which action research is founded have not been challenged, emancipatory, practical and technical action research are open to broad interpretations of its ideals. This has highlighted the problematic nature of action research with regards to social engineering. Consequently it has been shown that emancipatory action research, due to the fact that it has made the social researcher redundant, is not suited to the sphere of social inquiry within sport management. While technical and practical action research, due to the way they have been interpreted within a positivistic framework, do not provide a suitable and justifiable alternative methodology.

Chapter 7

Reflective Practices for Action and Engagement

Much research has become increasingly self reflexive and reflective. Such a change may be described by some as a narcissistic preoccupation—an introspective navel gazing that deflects from what is being argued to who is arguing it.

K.Plummer (2001: p. 205)

What is reflection?

In recent years there has been considerable interest in the notions of reflection and reflective practice in a number of professions such as nursing, teaching and management. The literature on the topic often traces the roots of those ideas to the work of Schon (1983), although other commentators (i.e. Habermas, 1973; Kolb, 1984) have influenced its development.

The value of the reflection in teaching and the need for preparing more reflective teachers are not new to the education literature (Calederhead, 1989; Gore, 1987; VanManen 1977; Zeichner and Liston 1987). Tsangaridou and Siedentop (1995) provide an extensive overview of practical and empirical efforts on reflection in classroom and physical education settings.

The belief that reflection is a prerequisite to learning from experience is a conclusion of the Centre of Creative Leaderships Research (Bunker and Webb, 1992; Lombardo, 1988). These researchers endorse the use of job experiences for developmental purposes. But even though they are optimistic about the future prospects of learning from experience, their *Lessons of Experience* book concludes on a note of frustration. 'It is staggering to think how much experience is wasted simply because managers aren't allowed, or forced to stop and make sense of what happened' (McCall, Lombardo and Morrison, 1988, p. 188). The frustration is two fold: (1) that many opportunities for real-time learning are missed, and (2) that a reason for this is that managers do not examine what happens to them in an experience, they fail to reflect.

Specific data on managers of business organisations demonstrate their inclination toward action over reflection. Mintzberg (1973) found this to be the case due to the fragmented, varied and unrelenting pace of managerial work. Kolb's (1984) work on learning styles discovered that managers show a preference for more active styles. That reflection is not something managers readily do has also been a finding of the Centre of Creative Leadership (McCall, Lombardo and Morrison, 1988). Finally, according to action research by Robinson and Wick (1992) the bottom-line orientation of most business organisations does not encourage reflection.

An emerging source of data on reflection in management is corporate management development programmes that include reflection as one of their objectives. Examples of reports of this action -type research include Argyris (1991), Marsick (1988) and Robinson and Wick (1992).

The importance of reflection is gaining recognition among management practitioners. A conclusion of a survey of best practices in executive development at 77 American companies was that executives need to be encouraged to approach learning opportunities in a more conscious and reflective way (Mann and Staudenmier, 1991). Management development programmes are now emerging that includes conscious reflection as an explicit objective (e.g., Marsick, 1990; Robinson and Wick, 1992). If theory, research and practice all recognize the importance of reflection to a managers' learning from experience, then why has it not received more attention by sport management researchers?

Sport management literature pays lip service to reflection but not much else. The intention of this chapter is to provide an account of the theoretical traditions of reflection and raise methodological issues and recommendations for the application of reflection in sport management settings.

Definitions of Reflection

Adler (1991) summarises three possible definitions. It can be taken to mean the ability to analyse one's own practice, the common-sense view. Alternatively, it can be defined as a process incorporating a problem setting approach and learning by doing. Finally, it can be defined as critical enquiry, which extends beyond technical expertise and focuses upon objectives, situational context and ethical issues. All incorporate ideas of critical enquiry but all possess unique features. Thus, any person wishing to encourage reflection must begin by specifying clearly what is intended by the use of the term.

The lack of certainty over definition has led to concerns over the use of reflection. In relation to reflective thinking versus reflective action there seems to be wide agreement that reflection is a special form of thought (McNamara, 1990). With regard to reflection and problem solving while there is some consensus that reflection is centrally concerned with finding solutions to real problems (Adler, 1991; Calederhead, 1989;) questions can be raised about whether solving problems should be considered an inherent characteristic of reflection. Some proponents would argue by their logic or practice that its essential nature is thinking about action.

The term critical reflection like reflection itself appears to be used loosely, some taking it to mean no more than constructive self-criticism of one's actions with a view to improvement. It can be argued, however, that the concept of critical reflection implies the acceptance of a particular ideology, along with its accompanying assumptions and epistemology (McNamara, 1990; Zeichner and Liston, 1987). Taken together these form a particular theoretical framework for reflection.

Critiques of reflection (Gore, 1987) often make use of the hierarchy outlined by Van Manen (1977) who proposed three levels derived from Habermas (1973). The first level, technical reflection is concerned with the efficiency and effectiveness of means to achieve certain ends, which themselves are not open to criticism or modification. The second practical reflection, allows for open examination not only of means, but also of goals, the assumptions upon which these are based and the actual outcomes. This kind of reflecting in contrast to the technical form recognises the meanings are not absolute, but are embedded in and negotiated through language. The third level critical reflection, as well as including emphases from the previous two, also calls for considerations involving moral and ethical criteria (Adler, 1991; Gore and Zeichner, 1991), making judgments about whether professional activity is equitable, just, and respectful of persons or not. In addition, critical reflection locates any analysis of personal action within wider socio-historical and politico-cultural contexts (Zeichner and Liston, 1987).

Origins of Reflection

Ever since the popularisation of Schon's (1983) seminal book reflective practice has been a constant theme among some groups of professionals. Yet reflection was no new idea when Schon wrote his book. Historically Dewey (1993) who himself drew on the ideas of many earlier educators such as Plato, Aristotle, Confucius, is acknowledge as a key originator in the twentieth century of the concept of reflection. He considered it to be a special form of problem solving, thinking to resolve an issue, which involved active chaining, a careful ordering of ideas linking each with its predecessors. Within the process consideration is to be given to any form of knowledge or belief involved and the grounds for its support. His basic ideas are seminal and indicate that reflection may be seen as an active and deliberative cognitive process involving sequences of interconnected ideas that take account of underlying beliefs and knowledge. Reflective thinking generally addresses practical problems allowing for doubt and perplexity before possible solutions are reached.

Freire (1972), Habermas (1973) and Mezirow (1978) had all been writing about reflection before Schon work was published. Freire for instance, discussed the relationship between reflection and action and argued that congruence's between the two are a form of praxis and there are certain similarities here to Argyri's (1976) and Schon's (1983) espoused theory and theory in use. Habermas had explored reflection in a variety of forms in his *Knowledge and Human Interests* in which he argues that self-reflection is a form of science, and here he combined critical sociology with Freudian analyses. Mezirow was influenced by Habermas and he produced a typology of reflection with seven different levels. Yet it was Schon's book, focussing as it does on the profession and professional practice, which attracted most attention.

In the organisation field Lewin (1951) wrote of reflection as that which reinforces learned behaviour and leads to new or higher-level abstractions. Lewin posited reflection as one of five elements in a cycle of learning from experience. Reflective observation and abstract conceptualisation are two components of Kolb's (1984; 1996) experiential learning theory. According to this theory, reflective observation entails understanding situations and their meaning through careful observation and description. There is an emphasis here on deliberation as opposed to action, on giving observations personal meaning. In short, reflective is knowledge of experience. Abstract conceptualisation involves formal hypothetico-deductive reasoning. The emphasis is on logic, ideas, and concepts, on thinking as opposed to feeling. In brief, abstract conceptualisation is knowledge about experience. Reflective observation and abstract conceptualisation are the perceptual and cognitive components of Kolb's learning cycle. They enable a person to make sense of a prior experience and then form concepts and generalizations to guide future action. Kolb's theory, including the validity of his Learning Style Inventory, which was developed to assess person's learning styles, is not without its critics (Allinson and Hayes, 1988; Freedman and Stumpf, 1980). Kolb's theory says little about reflective observation and abstract conceptualisation beyond defining them and positioning them within the learning cycle.

A theorist from the field of adult learning who has done considerable work with reflection is Mezirow (1991). The crux of learning to Mezirow is critical reflection, that is, critical assessment of the way one gives meaning to experiences. This requires surfacing and questioning that which is taken for granted. Such reflection can produce 'transformational' learning, which involves the formation of new more accurate mindsets that allow a more open, inclusive, discriminatory and integrative understanding of one's experiences. Although most learning is not of this type Mezirow believes that ultimately this is the only learning that really matters.

Argyris (1993) and his colleagues have written extensively on learning in organisations (Argyris, 1993; Argyris and Schon, 1978; Argyris, Putman and Smith, 1985). Argyris has long held that experience is the ultimate teacher: 'Self-insight and human skill in living can be learned only through living in and learning from, the stream of life events we call experience' (p. 218). The primary contribution of this work is the distinction between what is called single-loop and double-loop learning. Single-loop learning involves change within the context of existing premises and assumptions. If goals are not being met corrective action can be taken. But the goals and current operating procedures themselves are not questioned. In contrast, double-loop learning requires surfacing fundamental underlying assumptions and beliefs and then challenging them to determine if they are in the service of accomplishing desired goals.

Argyris (1996) does not use the term reflection in his writings, but it is clearly implied to be a prerequisite for the intense surfacing and questioning of fundamental underlying assumptions involved in double-loop learning. Learning at this deep level requires considerable cognitive effort and self-awareness. A major barrier to double-loop learning and by implication to reflection is defensive reasoning. Argyris claims that most managers act so as to avoid embarrassment or threat, and feelings of vulnerability or incompetence. This causes them to reason defensively, that is, to keep private and untested the premises, inferences and conclusions that drive their behaviour. Given this is the case; the open inquiry implied by reflection is something that would be perceived as intimidating by managers. Simply put, fear of not liking what they might see in their 'reflection' is a hindrance to reflecting and ultimately to double-loop learning.

Argyris' thinking highlights the important role of reflection in genuine learning as well as provides a reason why individuals find it difficult to learn reflectively. Marsick (1988) in drawing from Mezirow's and from Argyris' work, describes another aspect of reflection, which aimed at increasing personal awareness. She makes a distinction between critical reflectivity (which is essentially critical reflection or double-loop learning as defined by Mezirow and Argyris respectively) and reflectivity. The focus on reflectivity is self-understanding. According to Marsick, reflectivity is important not only for learning about one's self, but also for task-related learning since that learning is often embedded in social norms that impact on one's personal identity. Reflectivity is very similar to Hall's (1986) personal learning. What is important here is recognition that it is possible to reflect not only about the external world but about oneself as well. Reflection therefore has implications for the context of professional practice. Schon (1983; 1987) examines reflection in this context by analysing the way professionals (i.e. architects, psychotherapists, managers) go about the daily practice of their profession. However, approaches of this nature have had their greatest application in the training of teachers, but can be of significant interest for sport managers.

Schon's View of Professional Practice

In *The Reflective Practitioner* Schon (1983) stresses the idea of practical professional knowledge, which he terms 'knowledge-in-action'. He describes at length a process he terms 'reflection-in-action', by which knowledge-in-action develops in a manner that he argues can be as 'rigorous' as the development of theory in the 'scientific' research tradition. The uniqueness of Schon's contribution is two-fold and quite powerful in its potential. In addition to elaborating and richly illustrating with case studies the process of reflection-in-action, Schon (1) reviews the academic tradition in Western culture and reveals (2) how deeply rooted are our most basic assumptions about what counts as 'knowledge' and who speaks most authoritatively about that knowledge.

Schon (1983) illumes the distinction between the theoretical and the practical in his description of 'technical rationality', a model which assumes that professional knowledge comprises theories and concepts (systematic knowledge) which lead to the specification of general principles which can be applied to practice. Borne out of the increase specialisation of knowledge, and reinforced by the separation of research and practice technical rationality is, according to Schon, a dominant force throughout academia. He begins his thesis by challenging what he sees as the 'dominant epistemology of practice'.

> According to the model of Technical Rationality—the view of professional knowledge which has most powerfully shaped both our thinking about the professions and the institutional relations of research, education, and practice—professional activity consists in instrumental problem solving made rigorous by the application of scientific theory and technique (p. 21).

He continues that from the perspective of technical rationality professional practice focuses on problem solving. In other worlds, problems are recognised and are solved with reference to established theories. Schon (1983) criticises technical rationality on several grounds. He argues that it is deficient in its concentration on problem solving since this approach ignores problem setting. Professionals do not receive ready-made problems. From given situations they must analyse component parts and firstly construct the problem by trying to understand the situation, its uncertainties and confusions. Only after this can the problem be solved. Yet this is not necessarily a simple task either. Recourse to theory may not of itself yield a satisfactory solution. Schon (1983) argues that technical rationality cannot adequately accommodate practical competence in situations, which differ from those encountered during a course of instruction, but rather only works for situations that mirror what is taught. Thus, there will be situations where the practical problem will not match the theory.

> If problems of practice do not present themselves in a way, which allows the direct application of theory, then clearly theory cannot readily be mapped onto

practice. If we don't know what the problem is exactly then theory will hardly help us solve it (p. 203).

Post-qualification and away from university, sport management professionals are likely to encounter situations which do not fit the textbook examples. Judgement a presumed hallmark of professionalism is required, but it must be questioned how that judgment is developed. Schon (1983) argues that each professional builds up a set of experiences and draws on these to help in the task of problem solving. Theory is not ignored, but becomes intertwined with experience so that some sort of internalised understanding rather than pure theory is applied.

For this to happen Schon (1983) advocates a period of reflection where problem setting is a prelude to problem solving.

> They (professionals) are coming to recognize that although problem setting is a necessary condition for technical problem solving, it is not itseif a technical problem. When we set the problem, wc soloct what we will treat as the 'things' of the situation, we set the boundaries of our attention to it, and we impose upon it a coherence which allows us to say what is wrong and in what directions the situation needs to be changed. Problem setting is a process in which, interactively we name the things to which we will attend and frame the context in which we will attend to them (p. 40).

Schon (1983) cautions however, that it is not at all clear that the reflective process can achieve what is intends. The way in which professionals define a problem will to a large extent determine the solution. Thus, problem definition is not a neutral activity. Schon's alternative to technical rationality is, 'reflection-in-action'. Schon describes 'reflection-in-action' as 'an epistemology of practice implicit in the artistic, intuitive processes which some practitioners do bring to situations of uncertainty, instability, uniqueness and value conflict' (p. 49). When professionals say that they are 'thinking on their feet', 'keeping their wits about them' or 'learning by doing', they are reflecting-in-action. In other words, they are thinking as they act and displaying intuitive action. They may not be aware of this process, nor be able to describe it, but internally they are trying to make sense of a problem through reflection. Reflection-in-action implies that the professional thinks as he or she acts. For Schon this appears to be the ideal professional state, representing a critical awareness and powerful exercise of judgment.

Central to Schon's (1983) view of the professional practitioner is the ability to recognise and explore puzzling events that occur during the activities of practice. Thus the 'burned-out' practitioner is seen as one whose practice is 'repetitive and routine', neglectful of 'important opportunities to think about what he is doing' (p.61). He further states:

> ...if he learns, as often happens, to be selectively inattentive to phenomena that do not fit the categories of his knowing-in-action, then he may suffer from boredom or 'burn-out' and afflict his clients with the consequences of his narrowness and rigidity. When this happens, the practitioner has 'over learned' what he knows (p. 61).

Schon (1983) completes his introduction of 'reflection-in-action' by noting that our tendency to link professionalism with 'technical expertise' denies appropriate recognition of reflection-in-action as an important element of professional knowledge. The central portion of his book is devoted to showing how reflection-in-action can achieve greater recognition and use. His goals are challenging.

> The dilemma of rigor or relevance may be dissolved if we can develop an epistemology of practice which places technical problem solving within a broader context of reflective inquiry, shows how reflection-in-action may be rigorous in its own right, and links the art of practice in uncertainty and uniqueness to the scientist's art of research (p. 69).

One group of professionals Schon has studied are managers. Their reflection-in-action is basically similar to reflection-in-action in other professionals, but it also has special features of its own. The phenomena on which managers reflect-in-action are the phenomena of organisational life. The manager draws on an existing body of organisational knowledge (i.e. notions of mission and identity, facts about the task environment), adapting it to some present concern. The manager also serves as an agent of organisational learning, modifying in his present inquiry the body of knowledge that will be available for future inquiry by the organisation. Additionally, within an organisation the manager operates in a unique 'learning system' that may promote or inhibit reflection-in-action.

Schon (1983) claims that whereas managers readily reflect-in-action, they are much less inclined to reflect their reflection-in-action. The idea that reflection-in-action occurs in real-time when it can still make a difference to the situation at hand is what distinguishes reflection-in-action from other kinds of reflection. Indeed, what Burgoyne and Hodgson (1983) and what Mezirow (1991) call reflection, which involves pausing in the midst of action to think about what is happening or thinking back about what happened after the fact, Schon refers to as reflection-on-action. He does not deny the existence of this type of reflection. But he did find it to be less characteristic of professional behaviour than is reflection-in-action.

Schon's (1983) work represents a move away from strict theory towards a marrying of theory and practice, a move away from a hierarchical to a more equal relationship. It has also influenced the work of other educationalists including Usher and Bryant (1987), who argue that practice alongside Schon's idea of reflection-in-action can generate its own theory. The theory comes from being in a situation and shaping it through action selected from the results of reflection where 'knowledge emerges dynamically from the dialectical interchange between the subject and his action in practice situations' (p. 206). As such, Usher and Bryant argue that:

> ...the possibility therefore exists of a practice-derived knowledge, which is both experiential and rigorous. It can be seen as an alternative way to integrating theory and practice. Theory need not be abstract and remote from practice and the latter need not be intuitive and unsystematic (p. 206).

This implies that there is more than one kind of knowledge. Indeed Usher and Bryant (1987) argues that there are three kinds of knowledge: (1) theoretical knowledge, (2) technical knowledge/know-how and (3) practical knowledge/knowledge of how to act appropriately in the world—but that practical knowledge is the most appropriate in a professional context. This is because practical knowledge always exists in a situation or context, its purpose to generate 'informed and committed action' (p. 75), and it has an ethical dimension. The ethical dimension is of particular relevance given the need for sports managers to consider clients and other interest groups, for Usher argues:

> ...practical knowledge, since it is concerned with appropriate action in the world, must consider 'right' action. It is a kind of knowledge, which must inevitably take account of others, since those others are part of the situation (p. 76).

To illustrate consider ethical issues, which generally present the sport manager with a dilemma-whether to take the moral high ground or to give in to day to day commercial pressures. A period of reflection would allow the sport manager the opportunity of examining the dilemma in a situation removed from the immediacy of the commercial workplace. The sport manager would have the space to take the greater number of interests into account (for example, the public interest and the implications for the profession as a whole). Issues could be discussed which have only been superficially considered previously. The result could potentially (even if unlikely) be a more critical, questioning sport managers and one more likely to take a decision based on principle. But is this what the profession wants? A potential conflict may arise since the individual sport manager might be more certain, more dependable and less open to manipulation following reflection. However, the sport management profession as a whole might appear to be less certain, less predictable, and in the view of clients less dependable if members resort to individual principles for the resolution of conflicts and the collective bond or the generally accepted practice is weakened.

The implications of reflection may therefore extend beyond the individual sport manager. The best example here is the Tom Cruise movie character Jerry Maguire. Jerry reflects on his role as sports manager and writes a reflective business plan for Sport Management International based upon a client service focus. His colleagues and clients share, but do not support his reflective principles. Jerry is dismissed for his emancipatory stance. In this way, reflection operates for or against the cohesive nature of the profession depending upon whether it justified the status quo or challenged it.

Usher and Bryant (1987) conclude that emphasising practical knowledge bears both context and the practitioner's formalisation of knowledge (through reflection). The implications for the professional status of the practitioner are important for Usher claims that the practitioner will be seen as possessing wisdom, judgment and knowledge rather than merely being a technician. The ideas of Schon (1983), Usher and Bryant (1987) and Usher have the potential to:

- break down the dichotomy between theory and practice;
- raise the status of practical knowledge;
- draw on the experience of practitioners;
- provide a model for the consideration of ethical considerations; and
- encourage a more reflective approach.

Dimensions of Reflection

Three aspects of reflection are apparent when the various current thoughts on it are taken as a whole. These aspects can be thought of as three dimensions. These include (1) a dimension of time, (2) depth, and (3) orientation. Time refers to when in relation to an experience reflection occurs. It can occur antecedent to, concurrent with, or subsequent to an experience. An example of reflection before or antecedent to an experience is Kolb's (1984) abstract conceptualisation. Schon's (1983) reflection-in-action illustrates reflection during or concurrent with experience. And both Mezirow's (1991) critical reflection and Kolb's reflective observation are instances of reflection that happens after or subsequent to an experience. These theorists all believe implicitly at least that timing of reflective activity is an important aspect of the process of reflection.

The second dimension, depth, refers to the level at which reflective inquiry transpires. Three different levels are evident here: surface, subsurface, and core. Surface reflection is reflection aimed at understanding the basic meaning of an experience, as in Kolb's (1984) reflective observation and Mezirow's (1991) content reflection. Subsurface reflection is that which penetrates below the surface to expose underlying assumptions and beliefs. An example here is Argyris' (1982) double-loop learning. Finally, core reflection not only surfaces underlying assumptions but subjects them to critical reassessment as well. Mezirow's critical reflection and Argyris' double-loop learning illustrate reflection at this level. Some theorists' conceptions of reflection comprise multiple levels, as Argyris' double-loop learning and Schon's reflection-in-action do (reflection-in-action can happen at all three levels). The distinction between different degrees of depth of reflection is apparent in current writing on reflection.

A third dimension apparent in thinking about reflection is its orientation. Orientation has to do with that which reflection is directed toward. Following Kegan's (1982) theory of human development, the two directions apparent in current theory can be called object (that which is other than the self) and subject (the self). Most discussions of reflection deal with 'objects'. This involves reflecting on problems to be solved, tasks to be mastered, people to be understood and so on. This type of reflection is apparent in everyone who writes about reflection. Significantly less common is reflection directed at 'subject' or the self. Marsick's (1988) reflectively for self-understanding is illustrative of this aspect of reflection. Subsurface and core reflection may or may not be directed at the self.

The discussion of these three dimensions indicates the way in which reflection is currently viewed. Current views of reflection emanate from only a handful of theorists with Mezirow and Schon being the only ones who directly address reflection in any depth. Roth (1989) provides a comprehensive summary of the reflective practice processes (refer Table 1.1).

1.	Question what, why, and how one does things: ask what, why and how others do things.
2.	Seek alternatives.
3.	Keep an open mind
4.	Suspend judgment, wait for sufficient data, or self-validate.
5.	Compare and contrast
6.	Seek the framework, theoretical basis, underlying rationale (of behaviours, methods, techniques, programs).
7.	View from various perspectives.
8.	Identify and test assumptions (theirs and others, seek conflicting evidence.
9.	Put into different/varied contexts.
10.	Ask 'what if ...' ?
11.	Ask for others' ideas and viewpoints.
12.	Adapt and adjust to instability and change.
13.	Function within uncertainty, complexity and variety.
14.	Hypothesise.
15.	Consider consequences.
16.	Validate what is given or believed.
17.	Synthesise and test
18.	Seek, identify and resolve problems ('problem setting', 'problem solving').
19.	Initiate after thinking through (alternatives, consequences) or putting into context.
20.	Analyse—what makes it work: in what context would it not?
21.	Evaluate—what worked, what didn't, and why?
22.	Use prescriptive models (behavioural models, protocols) only when adapted to the situation.
23.	Make decisions in practice of the profession (knowledge created in use).

Source: Roth (1989, p. 32)

Table 1.1:A summary of the Reflective Practice processes.

Challenge to Reflection

Munby and Russell (1989) in an essay review of Schon (1983; 1987) question the lack of empirical testing of Schon's work, arguing that it is only by considerable empirical investigation that the importance on context of practice, the process of reflection itself and the consequences of reflection will be understood. This last point is particularly important given Adler's (1991) regret that there is as yet little empirical evidence that the strategies and teaching/learning situation adopted to encourage critical enquiry have worked.

Usher and Bryant (1987) suggest a further barrier to the adoption of reflection. They argue that the reflective approach is essentially an experimental one and as such is risky and unpredictable. Furthermore, even if willing to undertake reflection some sport practitioners may find it difficult to analyse their actions and thoughts or to articulate them. The implication here would seem to be that reflection is not necessarily an innate quality—there may be a need to teach how to be reflective in much the same way that communication or management skills can be taught. It seems therefore that much work still has to be done on how to encourage a reflective approach. In theory reflection may be desirable. If professions are treated as such because in addition to possessing knowledge and skills they are expected to exercise judgment and think critically and creatively, then reflection will keep these additional abilities alive. Additionally, professional judgment may be considered necessary to respond to new and unique situations.

Critical Theory and Reflection

This increasing interest 'in and on' practice has bee predominantly influenced by critical theory. Critical theory as utilized in this chapter refers to a body of work that derives from the Frankfurt School, a body of work grounded in the critique of dominant ideologies. Habermas (1973) is associated with this school and his theory of communicative action has been and continues to be the most prominent and influential in scholarship.

The ontological basis of critical theory requires an activist conception of the human being, who is capable of self-reflection. Human beings are regarded as being creative through the process of reflection. This process includes negotiation of dialogue with others and the creation of meanings of self and of others.

Critical theory discourse has been epitomised as one of mastery, autonomy and agency, and the practices so generated have been called the 'reflective doctrine'. It is claimed that those practices have transformed relationships and in an educational sense, provide for a curriculum revolution by dealing with the issue of transferring theory by integrating and applying academic knowledge to practice.

The so-called reflective doctrine prescribes activities and behaviour such as reflective processes in which practitioners are required to reflect continually upon the conditions of their actions. Feedback from sport management practitioners attest to the difficulties they experience in initiating and maintaining a reflective practitioner approach to their practice given the busy and tiring nature of their everyday work (Edwards, 1999).

The practitioners reported consistently that reflective sport management practice was not easy because it took energy, time, commitment and courage, and all of these things were in relatively short supply when they were perceived as being required in addition to the constraints of an already demanding work and personal life. For these sport management practitioners the battle for liberation in practice was a tedious, arduous and often relatively thankless one. Even given the personal and professional gains they also documented their feedback caused them to question whether the liberation that reflective process promises may be nothing more than a temporary pause from the constancy of power differentials entrenched inexorably in day-to-day sport management practice.

Critical theory and theorizing seeks to look into what is promoted as the status quo of various social contexts, to discover and expose the forces that maintain them for their particular advantages. As human social constructions, knowledge and social existence emerge out of identifiable human interests that serve certain purposes, which may be seen as immutable and inevitable, thereby maintaining as unquestioned the advantages of the powerful elite they favour.

The promises of critical theory that are either implied or made explicit in the reflective practitioner processes, relate to the nature of critical theory as a philosophical position and as a process of theorizing. There is a liberatory intent in using radical critiques to transform the existing restrictive social order and conditions within the status quo into those that are based and enacted on the principles of equality, freedom and justice. The emancipatory critique of critical theory relies on systematic reflection and promises freedom from the distorted understandings, communication and activities of pre-existing social structures thereby providing possibilities for new ways of being and acting within them.

Theory-Practice Divide

Fundamental to considerations of reflective practice is a consideration of sport management theory. Clarke, James and Kelly's (1996) discussion of reflective practice in a nursing context raised a number of issues that are applicable to management practice. They suggest that there are (1) different levels of theory, (2) knowledge is both personal and shared, (3) sharing of knowledge is important, (4) some knowledge is very recent, while some has a very long history, and (5) theory is dynamic. What appears obvious from their analysis is that sport management should be undertaking research into the nature of practitioner theory as is occurring in the fields like nursing, teaching and the core discipline of management.

Theory in sport management can be of two kinds. First, sport management theory provides the rationale appropriate for practice at the moment of acting in a particular context. When sport managers reflect in action they draw on their theories about sport management to generate the knowing in action. Second, there are theories about sport management. By reflecting on their practice and on formal professional development activities sport managers continually refine, revise and renew their personal practical knowledge, which contains their theories about sport management. These theories will have been developed from a wide range of sources.

Obviously sport management knowledge is in a sense personal knowledge since the knowing in action of sport management practice is created within the individual. However, the action takes place on the basis of a shared understanding of what is appropriate sport management practice. Many of the technical aspects of practice, the life world of sport managers and many of the aspects of the social, economic and political context of practice will be held conjointly with other sport managers. There will be a common understanding. However, some of an individual's knowing in action can never be shared with others except through the actions themselves because it is held almost at the intuitive level and can never be articulated. Also, as yet we know so little about the processes of reflection-in-action that it is not possible to say whether there is a shared understanding of them in the profession.

Given the nature of sport management theory it can be argued that any attempt to conceptualise reflection in professional practice must come from the experience of practitioners. What is now required is more research into the nature of practitioners' sport management theory.

Reflection in Sport Management Practice

Drawing upon critical theory Smyth (1991) proposed there are a number of key principles that ought to underpin reflective practice into sport management theory. He believed these were:

1. Reflection is founded on the belief that technical (knowledge) aspects of (sport management) practice are in a tentative and incomplete state. For example, the theory of sport management could all be described as technical knowledge. Reflection on this form of technical knowledge may lead to improvements in the efficiency and effectiveness of practice.

2. Reflection is fundamentally about the practical aspects of practice. This practical knowledge is the 'life-world' of sport management. The complex array of routines, rituals, roles and rules that make up the everyday experience of sport managers. Reflection in this area of knowledge is concerned with considering the appropriateness of action.

3. Reflection is a means to an end not an end in itself. Reflection produces some form of understanding or appreciation of learning experiences. The process of reflection cannot be divorced from the experience. This involves examining something new in relation to a practitioner's current understanding and then making changes to their practice.

4. Reflection is seen as an active process. It can be contrasted with responding to experience in a complacent, routinized, accustomed, unaware way. The kind of 'mindless' action that actually inhibits development. Reflection is viewed provisionally as the mechanism by which sport managers' extract learning from experience.

5. Reflection occurs best when it begins with the experiences of practitioners as they are assisted in the process of describing, informing, confronting and reconstructing their theories of practice.

6. Reflection is a process that is centrally concerned with challenging the dominant hegemonic beliefs and an ideology implicit in the way sport management is currently organised.

Reflection in this way allows power and knowledge domains to be available for scrutiny.

7. Reflection should not be restricted to practitioners reflecting individually upon their practice, there also needs to be collective and collaborative dimensions to it as well. The outcome for such reflection is for professionals to draw upon the vast array of collective knowledge in order to exercise professional judgment as they act individually.

8. Reflection should not be restricted to examining only technical knowledge. It should also be possible to critically reflect upon the social, political and economic context of practice. An outcome of reflection in this domain is the fundamental growth and transformation of the individual and increased liberation and emancipation.

Reflection 'in and on' practice has a range of different purposes. One purpose of reflection is to make sense of experience. Another purpose of reflecting during practice is for professionals to draw upon their knowledge in order to exercise professional judgement.

Reflective Research in Sport Management

The process of reflection particularly reflection-in-action is seriously under researched. The fact is that we know very little about it. Reflective research in sport management has the potential to make significant contributions to practice. At a general level reflective sport management research is intended to generate theory grounded in data, which explains the nature of the sport managers' reflection in learning from developmental experiences. Such theory simply does not exist at present.

The purpose of early research on reflection in sport management is to build theory rather than prove theory. Given that what is proposed is exploratory theory-building research the research questions should be intentionally open-ended. For example:

- How does reflection aid in the learning process?
- What variations are there in the reflective process?
- What are the consequences of reflection and non-reflection?
- What conditions inhibit reflection?

Researching these questions should go a long way toward increasing our understanding of the conditions in sport organisations and sport workplaces.

Although these questions require empirical investigation before complete answers can be provided it is possible to offer several propositions related to these questions. The tentative nature of these propositions cannot be overemphasised. Even so they play a valuable role in laying a foundation for proposed research. For example:

- Reflection is not a rational or systematic process for sport managers.
- Sport managers may be unaware on how they reflect.
- Sport managers may be unaware of their use of sport management theory.
- Reflection will be experienced in a variety of ways by different sport managers.
- Sport managers' life and/or career stage may affect the extent to which they engage in reflection.
- Sport managers at higher levels of management will be more likely to engage in reflection than those at lower levels.
- Reflection will result in future behaviour that is more deliberate.
- Certain sport organisations functions (i.e. research, marketing, strategic planning) will be more conducive to reflection than others (i.e. accounting, ticketing, seating).
- Sport organisations with a commitment to total quality management will be likely to be conducive to reflection.

Rationale for Reflection Research

The research methods used to investigate a given phenomenon should be chosen based upon the nature of the phenomenon and the extent of existing knowledge about it. Reflection in learning from experience is a complex and inexact if not messy activity.

Complex indeterminate context-bound social phenomena like reflection are best studied using what has been called 'inquiry from the inside' (Evered and Louis, 1981), 'direct research' (Mintzberg, 1979), or 'naturalistic inquiry' (Marsick, 1991), or ethnographic research. In contrast to the positivistic approach, which has historically characterised research of management development these approaches share the belief that organisational research should take a more involved, flexible, open-minded and contextually aware stance. Because qualitative methods are ideally suited to realising such a stance they are recommended for reflection. In addition to being useful for studying complex indeterminate phenomena in context, qualitative methods represent the most effective way to explore the social world from the perspective of the actors in that world.

Choice of method should also depend upon the state of knowledge of the issue under investigation. Theory testing through quantitative methods is typically called for when a substantial amount of research has already accumulated on a given subject. On the other hand, new research areas and those that have received minimal empirical attention are best addressed through theory building qualitative research (Glaser and Strauss, 1967). As suggested throughout this chapter, managerial reflection in learning from developmental experiences in sport organisations has received minimal direct empirical and theoretical attention of scholars. Thus the use of qualitative methods is appropriate. A research method that involves practitioners in their own reflective process is 'action research'.

Action Research and Reflective Practice

Critical theory has had an important influence on action research frameworks (i.e. Carr and Kemmis, 1986). It adds a further dimension to action theory by claiming that it is not enough to plan, act, observe and reflect within the given circumstances and constraints of an established system. These constraints may have to be critically analysed, debated and removed if they impede desired improvement, innovation and change. The quintessence for action research is the process of deliberation, the process of rational reflection and relentless criticism of all existing conditions and of the social milieu in which the group operates.

If this were applied to action research in sport management, the action researcher would identify a major problem or concern in their sport management practice. They would then design strategies for planned action, implement the strategic plan for action, observe and evaluate the action, reflect on the results of this evaluation and make the necessary changes required for the solution of the problem or for the first improvement step. This process would then be followed by a new cycle in the action research spiral.

Critical theory and action research has in common the notion of strategic action. This means an action is strategic when it is consciously and deliberately undertaken rather than on the basis of habit, custom, uncritical perception or hearsay. It requires practical judgment, recognition of extenuating circumstances and instant decisions. In contrast to mere behaviour, strategic action is constructed and justified not by 'objective' knowledge, principles and rules, but by 'personal knowledge', which is acquired through rational reflection on one's experience and strategic action.

Participative and collaborative research designs such as action research are seen to allow for reflection on the potential acquisition and the source of knowledge. Some action and participatory designs encourage reflection on ideological distortions of communication. The approach provides an empowering and emancipatory role for research.

Concluding Comments

This chapter has highlighted that reflective practice has come to be recognized as a core element of professional expertise. Reflective practice can refer to the ability to analyse one's own practice, the incorporation of problem solving into learning by doing, or the application of critical theory to the examination of professional practice. It has argued that all forms of reflection are vital to skilful sport management practice. It has further suggested that all forms of reflection provide unique opportunities to understand the practitioner's world and in doing so provide opportunities for emancipatory practice.

Chapter 8

Story, Narrative and Voice in Sport Management Research

> How to interpret stories and, more specifically, the texts that tell the stories, is at the heart of narrative analysis.
>
> Quinn Patton (1998: 118)

Introduction

A focus on narrative form emphasizes the intellectual affinities of sport management research with a group of theorists who have been vocal in their critique of the positivist and enlightenment assumptions. That is, that truth and power over nature will unfold progressively as the result of the utilisation of humanity's rational faculties—which continue to underpin most practice and research. What is sometimes called the 'counter-enlightenment' provides a welcome alternative tradition and source of validation. Drawing on such theorists as Jean-Pierre Lyotard (1984), who argues for narrative as an alternative mode of knowledge to science, and Jerome Bruner (1986) who demonstrates that narrative is a universal mode of cognition, narrative is currently enjoying unprecedented prestige. It is now seen as an avenue through which substantive meaning, or at least working knowledge can be developed.

Many writers who emphasise the modality of narrative also argue that all 'truth' is 'constructed' and therefore local and contingent. There is not one knowledge, but a variety of competing 'knowledges' each of which is developed within a specific cultural, professional or institutional framework. Emphasising the 'fictive', provisional and discursive aspects of all 'knowledge production', they draw on such sources as Kuhn's (1970) work on scientific paradigms and Foucault (1970) to dispute the outright truth claims of science.

Defining the Terms

It is important if story, narrative and voice are to become a genuine focus for sport management research inquiry that the meaning of each of these concepts is adequately defined and delimited. Narrative is from the Latin narratives. Story is 'Middle English', but ultimately derived from the Latin word 'historia'. Nevertheless in its contemporary usage 'story' is commonly used in more informal contexts that 'narrative' and quite often contains an element of provisionality.

Story and Narrative

The term story refers basically the 'to discussion of particular situations' (Clandinin, 1992, p.125). However, according to van Dijk (1993 p. 123) the relevant properties of stories are that:

- Stories are primarily about (past) human actions and cognition's although also descriptions of other events, objects, places or circumstances may be part of stories. For example, as conditioned or consequences to human action.
- Stories are usually about events and action that are (made) interesting for the audience. This 'pragmatic interestingness' is usually obtained by the account of events or actions that are unexpected, deviant, extra-ordinary or unpredictable, given the knowledge and beliefs of the audience.
- This also implies that stories are usually told to entertain the audience. For example, by influencing their aesthetic or emotional reaction. However, stories may also have broader social, political or cultural functions or play a role in the argumentative schema.
- Stories may be told from different perspectives or points of view, may feature the storyteller as a participant or not, and may be realistic or fictitious.

There is something impermanent, perishable and exploratory about a story. Stories are not always of course spoken, though the 'short story', the 'tale of detection', the yarn, terms that refer to literary forms, represent a sophisticated and specialized usage. Within the sport management research context stories are almost always less finished, less formal and less deliberated than the narrative. From this distinction some others follow. Stories and tales are casual, informal and contingent. Narratives are premeditated, organized, and formal and have a structure that is their own.

The term narrative—though it refers to spoken and informal discourse—reflects the professional and conceptual processes through which the original material (the story or stories) has been put. The real point of this distinction is that narratives should contain a reflective or theoretical component. It may not be overt, but the shaping and organization of a narrative would usually reflect and transmit the consequences of a meditative or generalizing process of thought. Narratives do not exist as Bruner (1991) writes:

> ...in some real world, waiting there patiently and eternally to be veridically mirrored in a text. The act of constructing a narrative moreover, is considerably more than selecting events either from real life, from memory, or from fantasy and then placing them in an appropriate order. The events themselves need to be constituted in the light of the overall narrative (p. 8).

To construct a narrative is to make an intervention into a field conceptualised (whether fully consciously or not is insignificant) as problematic. It is to address issues, though these are not addressed directly, but through the selection and arrangement of material.

Narrative is thus a reflective practice whereas story is not and because it is a reflective practice narrative is connected, as story is not, with authority. The 'narrator' is automatically endowed with power, with control over the material he or she presents, a power that flows to him or her through the position as organizer of the material. In moving from 'story' to 'narrative' it has become part of a reflective, self-conscious and interventionary process. In other words, to construct a narrative requires abstract thought. To write a narrative requires intellectual commitment and energy. Moreover, the construction of a narrative involves mediation upon social and ethical issues.

Voice

There is a related term that must be discussed—the term of 'voice'. Along with story and narrative it is presently in vogue, though this time its antecedents are not with 'postmodern theorists' but with the Russian literary critic and philosopher, Mikhail Bakhtin. Sometimes 'voice is used synonymously for 'story', at other times it means 'professional knowledge or orientation'. When one calls writing a 'voice' one is enlisting the residual power of this tradition to give power to the group or individual concerned. The term 'voice' tends to carry with it unconsciously the assumption that the group has a natural authenticity which is identical to itself, uncontaminated by the language and values of other usually more dominant groups.

But as Jacques Derrida (1981) insists, the meanings given by the living voice depend upon a process of differentiation between signs, in this case sound signs, as much as writing does. Speech can, no more than writing, be said to be a transparent medium of subjective experience. The term 'voice' lays claim to this by its own independent natural authority. But in fact no language is like this, and no voice is unproblematically free from or uncontaminated by the terms, values or concepts of others. When the term 'voice' is used in reference to what is in practice writing, we have a rhetorical trope whose complicated elision of these points is quite different from the supposed innocent directness that is simultaneously claiming. 'Voice' thus collaborates with 'story' in valorising that which is unpremeditated and apparently unmediated, but the term is in fact involved in quite complicated contestations and valorisations of meaning. It carries much the same meaning as 'representation' in the political sense, but without the separation between origin and signifier that 'representation' always insists upon.

As the story goes the narrative use of the individual's voice is perhaps one of the most important issues relating to research utilising the narrative perspective. Indeed, few traits of current biographies are more firmly entrenched than the conventional use of the individual's voice. Past research, (Altrichter, 1993; Goodson, 1991) has attempted to throw light upon the issue of the voices of marginalized groups within the society. In point of fact in recent years 'many researchers have become disenchanted with the academic process of noise reduction' by suppressing the more disturbing aspects of representing the individuality of human interaction. Academics such as (Ball, 1989) however, began to lead researchers to break down some of the established conventions of objectivity and highlight issues such as gender, race, homophobia, and socio-economic class by representing the marginalized voices within culture. Some would argue that at times Ball (1989) enters into a dialogue with the respondent. Consequently, a distinction must be drawn here between dialogue and voice. As Ruddick (1993) remarks:

Dialogue is a part of social convention where rules underwrite the possibility of speaking and being heard: turn taking offers more promise of equality (p. 8).

She continues by referring to voices being:

...emotive, more disembodied, more disturbing. At one level they can 'represent' individuals or groups who have been denied the right to contribute or who have simply not been heard (p. 8).

The issue of voice can be well represented by narrative writing and the use of narratives 'frequently embed exemplars-concrete, situated examples of action' (Witten, 1993, p. 107) as told by the marginalized individual. In this manner the stories of narrative are thus 'the stories of everyday life' (Clegg, 1993, p. 32) and more importantly the stories of everyday peoples voices, like those of sport managers.

Narratives 'are embedded so deeply in culture and everyday life' that it could be argued that the configuration of language indicates a profound pursuit for storytelling, which appears as a basic instinct common to all human life. Indeed, language utilised in narrative has become so sedimented and 'natural' in our daily experience that only rarely, if ever, do we consider how they construct, legitimate, and perpetuate a particular order of coherence and sense making. In sum narratives indicate a 'major discourse genre for reproduction' (van Dijk, 1993, p. 125) of individual or group voices.

Narrative and Reminiscing

When engaged in narrative research the researcher can be accused of using prior knowledge by reminiscing about his or her own life experiences. Sparkes (1995) refers to this process as 'narrative of self' (p. 175). In fact, 'the individual is not admitting to the self that he/she is denying the existence of things prior'. However, the self should be prepared to accept a situation of neutrality before the research begins. Consequently, the sport manager's life could be interpreted in the context of a narrative report and the act of reminiscing also becomes an important tool for representing the narrative of the manager's life. In other words, the act of reminiscing can have a major effect on the final production of the narrative. Furthermore, and perhaps more importantly, reminiscing is the precursor to reflection, which requires a deeper form of thought. Another form of interference in the narrative comes from the acceptance of nostalgia. This can also function as an important perspective in the act of reminiscing. Thus, the nostalgic or positive thoughts of the past may lead some respondents to reminisce and over-emphasise the nature of certain points in the narrative. When this happens, if the researcher has experienced similar occurrences, the passage of narrative might take on a stronger significance than warranted within the text. In short, nostalgia must therefore have some influence over the 'truth' of the narrative.

Narrative and Truth

Through the use of narrative language and dialogue researchers can make courageous and convincing pronouncements that can be camouflaged from finite inquiry and interrogation. Witten (1993) also believes this is true because of the 'cognitive and psychological effects of stories on listeners' (p. 105). It could be argued that narratives render the listener susceptible to having their attention caught by often provocative speech or through tone of voice, tense, and vivid and concrete details whereby plots and episodes are unfurled. Weaver and Dickson (1982) argue that 'through the use of linguistic features, attention is drawn to the exploits of the narratives as actors, the setting in which it occurs, and the consequences of the actor's behaviour' (p 256). The importance of these salient narratives is likely to be retained and persist over time, for as Martin (1982) suggests immediate language is memorable. Consequently, narratives can have a powerful impact and plausible persuasive effects on the listeners. In addition, the unparalleled strength of narrative talk stems from its ability to state claims of truth, which are shielded from testing or debate in the memorable and persuasive text. As Jefferson (1978) suggests the rules of narrative or story telling—the conventions of the game—make it difficult for a listener to question the narrative's content. Witten (1993) supports this comment by stating that:

> The presumption, encased in narrative, is shielded from testing or debate; it is a claim to validity that denies the need for justification or proof. In short, the narrative is a powerfully persuasive, presumed claim to truth and correctness that is not ordinarily subjects to challenge (p. 107).

So how can we be sure that the narrative has been written correctly and does not falsify the truth? It appears as though all the normal conventions of interpretative research are followed when writing the narrative cross checking by the use of triangulation and rereading by the subject can counteract any contradictions of the truth. However, if working in isolation or in a clandestine nature the narrative discourse utilised often relies on its 'truth' by the reputation of the writer. It is not our purpose in this chapter to discuss the nature of truth in academic research however; the concept would make an important contribution to the nature of interpretative research in our field and should be followed up vigorously.

Concluding Comments

This chapter has been a plea for clarity. Many writers who concentrate on 'story', 'narrative' and 'voice' do so as part of an argument against the mechanistic conceptions of management. In particular Bruner (1986, 1991) argue that narrative is a useful a way of approaching the world of sport management research. They go on to add that it is a useful a tool, and in many ways as useful to date as more scientific approaches. But these claims will carry little weight if these crucial terms are employed so loosely within the field. 'Story' is informal, provisional and exploratory. 'Voice' means the distinct epistemology of a social, professional and political group. 'Narrative' should mean the consciously formulated, premeditated and coherent account of an experience. When defined in this way, 'narrative' involves recognition of its author as capable, self-defining and intellectually able.

Sport management research narratives would mean not merely anecdotal, casual accounts, but involve a blending of theoretical with empirical or experiential materials. It is this capacity to connect theory with experience, to forego the relationship between daily practice and knowledge, that makes narrative a vital tool for the future of sport management research inquiry.

References

Alder, S. (1991). The reflective practitioner and the curriculum of teacher education. *Journal of Education for Teaching, 17*, (pp. 139–150).

Allinson, C. W., & Hayes, J. (1988). The learning styles questionnaire: An alternative to Kolb's inventory? *Journal of Management Studies. 25* (3), (pp. 269–281).

Alvesson, M. (1993a). *Cultural perspectives on organizations.* Cambridge: Cambridge University Press.

Alvesson, M., & Willmott, H. (1996). *Making sense of management: A critical analysis.* London: Sage.

Anderson, G. (1989). Critical ethnography in education origins: Current status and new directions. *Review of Education Research.* (53), (pp. 249–270).

Argyris, C. (1976). Theories of action that inhibit individual learning. *American Psychologist. September,* (pp. 638–654).

Argyris C., & Schon, D. A. (1978). *Organizational learning: A theory of action perspective.* Reading, MA: Addision-Wesley.

Argyris, C. (1982). The executive mind and double loop learning. *Organisational ...an,* (pp. 5–22).

...gyris, C., Putman, R., & Smith, D. M. (1985). *Action science.* San Francisco: Jossey-Bass.

Argyris, C., Putman, R., & McIain-Smith, D. (1990). *Action Science.* San Francisco: Jossey-Bass.

Argyris, C. (1993). *Knowledge for action.* San Francisco: Jossey-Bass.

Argyris, C. (1996). Skilled in competence. In K. Starkey (Ed.), *How organizations learn.* (pp. 81–91). London: International Thomson Business Press.

Auld, C. (1997). *Professionalisation of Australian Sport Administration: The effects of organisational decision making.* Belconnen, ACT: Australian Sports Commission.

Ball, S & Goodson, I. (1985). *Teachers lives and careers.* UK: Falmer Press.

Ball, S. (1989). *The Micro-politics of teaching.* UK: Falmer Press.

Bauman, Z. (1991). *Modernity and ambivalence.* Cambridge: Polity Press.

Bauman, Z. (1995). Searching for a centre that holds. In M. Featherstone (Ed.), *Global modernities* . London: Sage. (pp. 140–153)

Benson, J. K. (1977). Organisations: A dialectical view. *Administrative Science Quarterly. 22,* (pp. 1–21).

Berstein, R. J. (1976). *The restructuring of social and political theory.* Oxford: Blackwell.

Berstein, R. (1978). *The restructuring of social and political theory.* Philadelphia: University of Pennsylvania Press.

Best, S., & Kellner, D. (1991). *Postmodern theory: Critical interrogations.* London: Macmillian.

Bhaskar, R. (1979). *The possibility of naturalism.* Brighton: The Harvester Press.

Brew, A. (2001). The nature of research: Inquiry into academic contexts. London: Routledge Falmer.

Bronner, S. E. (1994). *Of critical theory and its theorists.* Cambridge: Blackwell.

Bruner, J. (1986). *Actual minds, possible worlds.* Cambridge, Mass. Harvard University Press.

Bruner, J. (1991), Acts of meaning, Cambridge, Mass. Harvard University Press.

Bunker, K. A., & Webb, A. D. (1992). *Learning how to learn from experience: Impact of stress and coping.* (p. 154). Greensboro. NC: Centre for Creative Leadership.

Burawoy, M., Ferguson, A., Fox, A. A., Gamson, K. J., Gartell, J., Hurst, N., Kurzman, L., Salzenger, C., & Schiffman, J. W. B. (1991). *Ethnography unbound: Power and resistance in the modern metropolis.* Berkeley, California: University of California Press.

Burgoyne, J. G., & Hodgson, V. E. (1983). Natural learning and managerial action: A phenomenological study in field setting. *Journal of Management Studies. 20* (pp. 387–399).

Burrell, G., & Morgan, G. (1979). *Sociology of paradigms and organisational life: Elements of the sociology of corporate life.* London: Heinemann.

Burrell, G., & Morgan, G. (1979). *Sociological paradigms and organizational analysis.* Aldershot: Gower.

Calederhead, J. (1989). Reflective teaching and teaching education. *Teaching and Teaching Education. 5*, (pp. 43–51).

Callinicos, A. (1989). *Against postmodernism: A Marxist critique.* Cambridge: Polity Press.

Carr, W., & Kemmis, S. (1986). *Becoming critical: Education, knowledge and action research.* Victoria: Deakin University.

Carr, W. (1995). *For education: Towards a critical educational inquiry.* Buckingham: Open University Press.

Chalip, L. (1996). Critical policy analysis: The illustrative case of New Zealand sport policy development. *Journal of Sport Management, 10* (3), (pp. 310–324).

Chalip, L. (1997). Action research and social change in sport: An introduction to the specisl issue. *Journal of Sport Management. 11* (1), (pp. 1–7).

Clandenin, D. J. & Connolly, F. M. (1994) Personal experience methods. In N. K. Denzin & Y. S. Lincoln (Eds.), *Handbook of qualitative research.* Thousand Oakes, California: Sage Publications.

Clarke, B., James, C., & Kelly, J. (1996). Reflective practice: Reviewing the issues and refocusing the debate. *International Journal of Nursing Standards. 33*, (pp. 171–180).

Codrescu, A. (1986). *A craving for swan.* Columbus: Ohio State University Press.

Connerton, P. (1980). *The tragedy of enlightenment.* Cambridge: Cambridge University Press.

Cuskelly, G. (1995). The influence of committee functioning on organizational commitment of volunteer administrators in sport. *Journal of Sport Behaviour. 18* (4), (pp. 254–269).

Deetz, S., & Kersten, A. (1983). Critical models of interpretative research. In L. Putnam & M. Pacanowsky (Eds.), *Communication and organizations.* Beverly Hills, California: Sage.

Delamount, S., & Atkinson, P. (1980). The two traditions in educational ethnography: Sociology and anthropology compared. *British Journal of Sociology of Education. 1* (2), (pp. 139–152).

Deleuze, G., & Guattari, F. (1994). *What is Philosophy?* (G. B. H. Tomlinson, Trans.). New York: Columbia University Press.

Denzin, N. (1988). Act, language, and self in symbolic interactionist thought. *Studies in Symbolic Interaction. 9*, (pp. 51–80).

Derrida, J. (1976). *Of grammatology.* (G. C. Spivak, Trans.). Baltimore: John Hopkins University Press.

Derrida, J. (1978). *Writng and difference.* (A. Bass, Trans.). Chicago: The University of Chicago Press.

Derrida, J. (1979). *Scribble (Writing-power).* Yale: French Studies.

Derrida, J. (1981). *Positions* (A. Bass, Trans.). Chicago: University of Chicago Press.

Derrida, J. (1982). *Margins of philosophy.* London: Harvester.

Derrida, J. (1983). The principal of reason: The university in the eyes of its pupils. *Diacritics, Fall,* (pp. 3–20).

Derrida, J. (1986). *Glass* (J. Leavy & R. Rand, Trans.). Lincoln, NB: University of Nebraska Press.

Derrida, J. (1987). *The postcard: From Socrates to Freud and beyond.* (A. Bass, Trans.). Chicago: University of Chicago Press.

Dewey, J. (1993). *How we think.* Chicago: Regnery.

Dick, B. (1992). Qualitative action research: Improving rigour and economy. In C. S. Bruce & A. L. Russell (Eds.), *Transforming tomorrow today.* (pp. 432–435). Brisbane: Ron Passfield.

Dick, B. (1993a). *Convergent interviewing: Version 3.* Brisbane: Interchange.

Dick, B. (1993b). *You want to do an Action Research thesis?: How to conduct and report action research.* Brisbane: Interchange.

Dick, B. (1995). *Action research and evaluation online.* Aerol. Available: <aerol-r-l@scu.edu.au [2001, Feburary 9].

Dick, B. (1997). *Action research and evaluation online: Session 4: Stakeholders and participation.* Aerol 5. Available: <areol-r-l@scu.edu.au [2000, March 17].

Eagleton, T. (1987, February 20). Awakening from modernity. *Times Literary Supplement.*

Edwards, A. (1999). Reflective practices in sport management. *Sport Management Review. 2* (1), (pp. 67–81).

Eliot, T. S. (1943) In N. Cherry (1999). *Action research: A pathway to action, knowledge and learning.* Melbourne: RMIT University Press.

Evered, R., & Louis, M. R. (1981). Alternative perspectves in the organisational sciences: Inquiry from the inside and inquiry from the outside. *Academy of Management Review. 6* (3), (pp. 385–395).

Fay, B. (1975). *Social theory and political practice.* London: Allen and Unwin.

Featherstone, M. (1988). In pursuit of the postmodern: An introduction. *Theory, Culture and Society. 5*(2), (pp. 195–215).

Featherstone, M. (1991). *Consumer culture and postmodernism.* London: Sage.

Fine, G. A., & Martin, D. D. (1995). Humor in ethnographic writing: Sarcasm, satire, and irony as voices in Erving Goffman's asylums. In J. V. Maanen (Ed.), *Representation in ethnography.* (pp. 165–197). Thousand Oaks, California: Sage.

Firat, A. F. (1992). Postmodernism and the marketing organisation. *Journal of Organisational Change. 5* (1), (pp. 79–83).

Fischer, F., & Surianni, C. (Eds.), (1984). *Critical studies in organization and bureaucracy.* Philadelphia: Temple University Press.

Forester, J. (1993). *Critical theory, public policy and planning practice.* Albany: University of New York Press.

Foss, S. K., & Gill, A. (1987). Michel Foucault's theory of rhetoric as epistemic. *Western Journal of Speech Communication, 51,* (pp. 384–401).

Foucault, M. (1970). *The order of things.* London: Tavistock.

Foucault, M. (1972). *The archaeology of knowledge.* London: Tavistock.

Foucault, M. (1977). *Discipline and Punish.* (A. Sheridan, Trans.). London: Allen Lane.

Foucault, M. (1978). Politics and the study of discourse, ideology and consciousness. In G. Burchell, C. Gordon, & P. Miler (Eds) The Foucault effect: Studies in Govern mentality London: Harvester Wheatsheaf, (pp. 53–72).

Foucault, M. (1980). *Power/knowledge selected interviews and other writings, 1972–77.* (C. Gordon, Trans.). New York: Harvester Wheatsheaf.

Foucault, M. (1981). The order of discourse. In R. Young (Ed.), *Untyping the text. .* London: Methuen, (pp. 48–78)

Foucault, M. (1983). The subject and power. In D. Dreyfus & P. Rabinow & M. Foucault (Eds.), *Beyond structuralism and hermeneutics.* (2nd ed.). Chicago: University of Chicago Press.

Fraser, N. (1989). *Unruly practices: Power, discourse and gender in contemporary social theory.* Cambridge: Polity Press.

Freedman, F. D., & Stumpf, S. A. (1980). Learning style theory: Less than meets the eye. *Academy of Management Review. 5,* (pp. 445–447).

Freeman, H., & Jones, A. (1981). Educational research and the two traditions of epistemology. *Educational Philosophy and Thoery. 12,* (pp. 1–20).

Freire, P. (1972). *Pedagogy of the oppressed.* Harmondsworth, UK: Penguin.

Frost, P. J. (1980). Toward a radical framework for practicing organizational science. *Academy of Management Review. 5,* 501–509.

Geertz, C. (1973). *The interpretation of cultures: Selected essays.* New York: Basic Books.

Giddens, A. (1979). *Central problems in social theory.* London: Macmillan.

Giddens, A. (1987). *Structuralism, poststructuralism and the production of culture.* Cambridge: Polity Press.

Giroux, H. A. (1992). *Border crossing: Cultural workers and the politics of education.* New York: Routledge.

Gitlin, A., Siegal, M., & Boru, K. (1989). The politics of method: From leftist ethnography to educative research. *Qualitative Studies in Education. 2,* (pp. 233–237).

Glaser, B., & Strauss, A. (1967). *The discovery of grounded theory: Strategies for qualitative research.* New York: Aldine.

Goodson, I. F. (1991). *Studying teacher's lives.* Routledge, London.

Gore, J. (1987). Reflecting on reflective teaching. *Journal of Teacher Education. 28* (2), (pp. 235–265).

Gore, J., & Zeichner, K. (1991). Action research and reflective teaching in pre-service teacher education: A case study from the United States. *Teaching and Teaching Education. 7,* (pp. 119–136).

Grimley, J. (1986). Critical educational policy analysis: A discussion of perspectives. *Australian Journal of Teacher Education. 11* (2), (pp. 19–25).

Habermas, J. (1971). *Knowledge and human interests.* (J. J. Shapiro, Trans.). Boston: Beacon Press.

Habermas, J. (1972). *Knowledge and Human Interests.* London: Heinemann.

Habermas, J. (1973). *Knowledge and human interests.* (2nd ed.). London: Heinemann.

Habermas, J. (1978). *Knowledge and human interests.* (J. J. Shapiro, Trans.). Cambridge, U.K.: Polity Press.

Habermas, J. (1984). *The theory of communicative action: Reason and rationalisation of society.* (T. McCarthy, Trans. Vol. 1). London: Heinemann.

Habermas, J. (Ed.). (1987). *The philosophical discourse of modernity.* Cambridge: Polity Press.

Habermas, J. (1987). *The theory of communicative action: Lifeworld and system.* (T. McCarthy, Trans. Vol. 1). Boston: Beacon.

Hall, D. T. (1986). Delemmas in linking succession planning to individaul executive learning. *Human Resource Management. 25,* (pp. 235–265).

Hammersley, M. (1992). *What's wrong with ethnography: Methodological explorations.* London: Routledge.

Hardy, C., & Clegg, S. R. (1997). Relativity without relativism: Reflexivity in post-paradigm organizational studies. *British Journal of Management. 8,* (pp. 5–17).

Hargreaves, A. (1994). *Changing teachers changing times: Teacher's work and culture in the postmodern age.* London: Sage.

Harpham.

Harvey, D. (1989). *The condition of postmodernity: An enquiry into the origins of cultural change.* Oxford: Blackwell.

Held, D. (1980). *An introduction to critical theory*. Berkeley, California: University of California Press.

Hesse, M. (1982). Science and objectivity. In J. B. Thompson & D. Held (Eds.), *Habermas: Critical debates*. London: Macmillan, (pp. 98–115).

Hoy, D., & McCarthy, T. (1994). *Critical theory*. Cambridge: Blackwell.

Hudson, W. (1989). *Postmodernity and continued social thought in lossmar: Politics in social theory*. London: RKP.

Huyssen, A. (1990). Mapping the postmodern. In L. Nicholson. (Ed.), *Feminism/Postmodernism* New York: Routledge, (pp. 234–280).

Jencks, C. (1987). *Post-modernism: New classicism in art and architecture*. New York: Rizzoli.

Jennings, L. E. (1995). Prisioners of our own perspectives: Recasting action research in modern/postmodern times. *Studies in Continuing Education. 17* (1&2), (pp. 78–85).

Kegan, R. (1982). *The evolving self: Problem and Process in Human Development*. Cambridge, MA: Harvard University Press.

Kellett, P. (1999). Organisational leadership: Lessons from the coaches. *Sport Management Review. 2* (2), (pp. 150–171).

Kemmis, S. (1985). Action research and the politics of reflection. In D. Boud & R. Keogh & D. Walker (Eds.), *Reflection: Turning experience into learning*, London: Kegan Page, (pp. 139–165).

Kemmis, S. (1991). Emancipatory action research and postmodernisms. *Curriculum Perspectives, 11* (4), (pp. 59–65).

Kemmis, S. (1995, May 26). *Research and communicative action*. Paper presented at the Invited Address: National Forum of the Innovative Project, Melbourne.

Kilduff, M., & Mehra, A. (1997). Postmodernism and organizational research. *Academy of Management Review. 22* (2), (pp. 453–480).

Kolb, D. A. (1984). *Experiential learning: Experience as a source of learning and development*. Englewood Cliffs. NJ: Prentice-Hall.

Kolb, D. A. (1996). Management and the learning process. In K. Starkey (Ed.), *How organizations learn*, London: International Thomson Business Press, (pp. 270–277).

Kuhn, T. (1962). *The structure of scientific revolutions*. Chicago: University of Chicago Press.

Kuhn, M., Long, C. & Quinn, L. (1991). *No stone unturned: The life and times of Maggie Kuhn*. Ballentine Books, New York.

Kusch, M. (1991). *Foucault's strata and fields: An investigation into archaeological and genealogical science studies*. Dordrecht: Kluwer Academic Publishers.

Layder, D. (1994). *Understanding social theory*. London: Sage.

Lewin, K. (1951). *Field research in social sciences*. New York: Harper and Row.

Linstead, S. (1993). Deconstruction in the study of organizations. In J. Hassard & M. Parker (Eds.), *Postmodernism and organizations*. Newbury Park, California: Sage, (pp. 49–70).

Linstead, S. (1993a). From postmodern anthropology to deconstructive ethnography. *Human Relations. 46* (1), (pp. 97–117).

Lombardo, M. M. (1988). How successful executives develop. In M. London & E. Mane (Eds.), *Career growth and human resource strategies*. New York: Quorum Books, (pp. 257–270).

Lukacs, G. (1971). *History and class consciousness*. Cambridge: MIT Press.

Lyotard, J. F. (1984). *The postmodern condition: A report on knowledge*. Manchester: Manchester University Press.

MacTaggart, R. (1989). *Principles for participatory action research.*, Deakin University.

MacTaggart, R. (1991). Action research is a broad movement. *Curriculum Perspectives. 11* (4), (pp. 44–47).

Mann, R. W., & Staudermier, J. M. (1991). Strategic shifts in executive development. *Training and Development. 45* (7), (pp. 37–40).

Marshall, J. D. (1989). Foucault and Education. *Australian Journal of Education, 33*, (pp. 99–113).

Marsick, V. J. (1988). Learning in the workplace: The case for reflectivity and critical reflectivity. *Adult Education Quarterly. 38* (4), (pp. 187–198).

Marsick, V. J. (1991). Action learning and reflection in the workplace. In J. Mizirow (Ed.), *Fostering critical reflection in adult-hood*, San Francisco: Jossey-Bass (pp. 23–46).

Martin, J. (1990). Deconstructing organisational taboos: The supression of gender conflict in organisations. *Organisational Science. 1* (4), (pp. 339–359).

Martin, J. Feldman. M. S. Hatch, M. J. & Sitkin, S. (1982). The uniqueness paradox in stories. *Administrative Science Quarterly.* 28. (pp. 438–453).

McCall, M., Lombardo, M. M., & Morrison, A. M. (1988). *The lessons of experience: How successful executives develop on the job.* Lexington, MA.: D.C. Heath.

McNamara, D. (1990). Research of teachers thinking: Its contribution to educating student teachers to think critically. *Journal of Education for Teaching. 16*, (pp. 147–160).

McNeil, P. (1990). *Research Methods.* London: Routledge.

Mezirow, J. (1978). *Education for perspective transformation: Re-entry programs in community colleges.* New York: Columbia University's Teacher's College.

Mezirow, J. (1991). *Transformation dimensions in adult learning.* San Francisco: Jossey-Bass.

Mintzberg, H. (1973). *The nature of managerial work.* New York: Harper and Row.

Mintzberg, H. (1979). An emerging strategy of direct research. *Administrative Science Quarterly. 24* (pp. 580–589).

Mulkay, M. J. (1985). *The word and the world: Explorations in the form of sociological analysis.* London: Allen and Unwin.

Munby, H., & Russell, T. (1989). Educating the reflective teacher: An essay review of two book by Donanld Schon. *Journal of Curriculum Studies. 21* (1), (pp. 71–80).

Opie, A. (1992). Qualitative research, appropriation of the other and empowerments. *Feminist Review. 40*, (pp. 52–69).

Packwood, A., & Sikes, P. (1996). Adopting a postmodern approach to research. *Qualitative Studies in Education. 9* (3), (pp. 335–345).

Parker, M. (1992). Post-modern organizations or postmodern organization theory. *Organization Studies. 13* (1), (pp. 1–17).

Parson, C. (1994). The impact of postmodernism on research methodology. *Nurse Inquiry. 2*, (pp. 22–28).

Plummer, K. (2001). *Documents of life: An invitation to critical humanism.* New York: Sage.

Porter, J.R. & R.E. Washington (1993). Minority identity and self-esteem. *Annual Review of Sociology.* 19, (pp. 139–161).

Prior, L. (1988). The architecture of the hospital: A study of spatia; organization and medical knowledge. *The British Journal of Sociology.* (pp. 86–113).

Prunty, J. (1985). Signposts for a critical educational policy analysis. *Australian Journal of Education. 29* (2), (pp. 133–140).

Quinn Patton, M. (1998). *Qualitative research and valuation methods.* (3rd ed.). London: Sage.

Rajchman, J. (1985). *The freedom of philosophy*. New York: Columbia University Press.

Rapoport, R. N. (1970). Three dilemmas in action research. *Human Relations. 23* (6), (pp. 499–513).

Ray, M., & Rinzler, A. (Eds.), (1993). *The new paradigm in business: Emerging strategies leadership and organisational change*. (World Business Academy ed.), New York: Tarcher/Perigee.

Ricouv, P. (1988). *Time and narrative. Vol III*. Chicago: University of Chicago Press.

Robinson, G. S., & Wick, C. W. (1992). Executive development that makes a business difference. *Human Resource Planning. 15* (1), (pp. 63–76).

Robinson, G. S., & Wick, C. W. (1992). Executive development that makes a business difference. *Human Resource Planning, 15* (1), (pp. 63–76).

Roth, R. (1989). Preparing the reflective practitioner: Transforming an apprentice through dialectic. *Journal of Teacher Education. 40* (2), (pp. 31–38).

Sarantakos, S. (1993). *Social research*. Melbourne: MacMillan.

Schon, D. A. (1983). *The reflective practitioner: How professional think in action*. New York: Basic Books.

Schon, D. A. (1987). *Educating the reflective practitioner: Toward a new design for teaching and learning in the professions*. San Francisco: Jossey-Bass.

Schwab, D. (1999). *Research methods for organisational studies*. Mahwah, NJ: Lawrence Erlbaun Associations.

Sharp, R., & Green, A. (1975). *Education and social control*. London: Routledge and Kegan Paul.

Sherry, J. F. (1991). *Postmodern alternatives: The interpretative turn in consumer research*.In T. S. Robertson & H.H. Kassarjian (Eds.), *Handbook of consumer behaviour (pp. 548-591) Englewood Cilffs, New Jersey*.

Shilbury, D. (1994). *A study of the strategic planning practices of the Australian football league clubs*. Unpublished doctoral dissertation, Monash University, Melbourne.

Skinner, J., Stewart, B., & Edwards, A. (1999). Amateurism to professionalism: Modelling organisational change in sporting organisations. *Sport Management Review. 2* (2), (pp. 173–192).

Smart, B. (1993). *Postmodernity*. London: Routledge.

Smircich, L., & Calas, M. B. (1987). Organizational culture: A critical assessment. In F. M. Jablin & L. L. Putnam & K. H. Roberts & L. W. Porter (Eds.), *Handbook of organizational communication: An interdisciplinary perspective*, Newbury Park, California: Sage, (pp. 228–263).

Smith, D. (1987). *The everyday world as problematic: A feminist sociology*. Boston: Northeastern University Press.

Smith, R. & Wexler, P. (1995). *After postmodernism: Education, politics and identity*. London: The Falmer Press.

Smyth, J. (1991). *Teachers as collaborative learners: Challenging dominant forms of supervision*. Milton Keynes: Open University Press.

Sparkes, A. (1995). Life histories and the issue of voice: reflections on an emerging relationship. *International Journal of Qualitative Studies in Education. 7*, (pp. 165–183).

Spindler, G., & Spindler, L. (1971). Foreword. In Rosefeld (Ed.), *Shut those thick lips: A study in slum school failure*. New York: Holt, Rinehart and Winston.

Thompson, J. B. (1983). Rationality and social rationalisation: An assessment of Habermas's theory of communicative action. *Sociology. 17*, (pp. 278–294).

Thompson, P. (1993). Postmodernism: Fatal distraction. In J. Hassard & M. Parker (Eds.), *Postmodernism and organizations*. (pp. 183–203). Newbury Park, California: Sage.

Tripp, D. (1993). *Critical incidents in teaching: Developing professional judgement*. London: Routledge.

Tyler, S. (1983). Ethnography, intentionally and the end of description. *American Journal of Semiotics. 3*, (pp. 83–98).

Tyler, S. (1987). *The unspeakable: Discourse, dialogue, and rhetoric in the postmodern world.* Madison, Wisconsin: The University of Wisconsin Press.

Usher, R. S., & Bryant, I. (1987). Re-examining the theory-practice relationship in continuing professional education. *Studies in Higher Education, 12* (2), (pp. 201–212).

Van Manen, M. (1977). Linking ways of knowing with ways of being practical. *Curriculum Inquiry. 6*, (pp. 205–228).

Van Mansen, M. (1990). *Researching lived experience: Human science for an action sensitive pedagogy.* State University of New York: Basic Books.

Venkatesh, A. (1989). Modernity and postmodernity. In T. Childers (Ed.), *Marketing theory and practice*, Chicago: American Marketing Association, (pp. 99–104).

Venkatesh, A. (1992). Postmodernism, consumer culture and the society of the spectacle. In J. F. Sherry. & B. Sternthal. (Eds.), *Advances in consumer research.* (Vol. xix, pp. 199–202). Provo, UT: Association of Consumer Research.

Wallace, R. & Wolf, A. (1986). *Contemporary sociological theory: Continuing the classical tradition* (2nd ed.). New Jersey: Prentice Hall.

Waters, M. (1994). *Modern sociological theory*. London: Sage.

Weber, M. (1978). *Economy and society: An outline of interpretive sociology.* Berkley, California: University of California Press.

Weedon, C. (1987). *Feminist practice and poststructuralist theory.* Oxford: Blackwell.

White, S. K. (1988). *The recent work of Jurgen Habermas: Reason, justice and modernity.* New York: Cambridge University Press.

Whyte, W. F. (1991b). Participatory action research: Through practice to science. In W. F. Whyte (Ed.), *Social research in participatory action research.* California: Sage (pp. 19–55).

Wilcox, K. (1980). *The enthnography of schooling: Implications for educational policy making.* (Project Report 80–A10): Institute for Research on Educational Finance and Governance.

Willmott, H. (1993). Strength is ignorance, slavery is freedom: Managing culture in modern organizations. *Journal of Management Studies. 30* (4), (pp. 515–552).

Witten, M., (1993). Narrative and the culture of the workplace. In D. M. Mumby (Ed.), *Narrative and social control: Critical perspectives*, California: Sage Publications (pp. 7–118).

Wolcott, H. (1975). Criteria for an ethnographic approach to research in schools. *Human Organisation. 24* (2), (pp. 111–127).

Woods, P., & Hammersley, M. (1977). Introduction: School experience: Explorations in the sociology of education. In P. Woods & M. Hammersley (Eds.), *School experience: Explorations in the sociology of education.* . London: Croom Helm, (pp. 9–27).

Zeichner, K., & Liston, D. (1987). Teaching student teachers to reflect. Harvard Education Review. 57, (pp. 23–48).

Index